MARK:
THE *Good News Preached* TO THE *Romans*

Phillip J. Cunningham, CSP

PAULIST PRESS
New York and Mahwah, N.J.

Cover design by Tim McKeen.

Library of Congress Cataloging-in-Publication Data

Cunningham, Phillip J., 1922-
    Mark : the good news preached to the Romans / by Phillip J. Cunningham.
        p. cm.
    ISBN 0-8091-3554-X
    1. Bible. N.T. Mark—Study and teaching. 2. Bible. N.T. Mark—History of contemporary events. 3. Bible. N.T. Mark—History of Biblical events. 4. Church history—Primitive and early church, ca.
    30-600. I. Title.
    BS2585.5.C86   1995   94-41670
    226.3'067—dc20   CIP

Published by Paulist Press
997 Macarthur Boulevard
Mahwah, NJ 07430

Printed and bound in the
United States of America

CONTENTS

CHAPTER THREE: CHRISTIANITY IN ROME

CHAPTER FOUR: MARK'S CHRISTIANS

CHAPTER FIVE: LEADERSHIP AND RIVALRY

CHAPTER SIX: THE PAROUSIA AND THE SON OF MAN

CHAPTER NINE: THE WONDERWORKER

CHAPTER TEN: THE TEACHER AND HIS TEACHINGS

CHAPTER ELEVEN: THE HOLY WEEK
PART ONE: SUNDAY TO TUESDAY

CHAPTER TWELVE: THE HOLY WEEK
PART TWO: WEDNESDAY AND THURSDAY

CHAPTER THIRTEEN: THE HOLY WEEK
PART THREE: FRIDAY TO SUNDAY

CHAPTER FOURTEEN: AFTERWORD

Dedicated in gratitude to my teachers and fellow Paulists:

EUGENE MICHAEL BURKE (1911-1984)
BENJAMIN BRIDGES HUNT (1919-1986)
JOHN ARTHUR CARR

"The man who can make hard things easy is the educator."
— *Ralph Waldo Emerson*

Prologue

THE BREAKING OF THE BREAD

It is Rome in the summer of 822 A.U.C.[1] (69 C.E.[2]). If the population of the capital city is a bit on edge, it is not surprising. After Emperor Nero's suicide in June of last year units of the Roman armies have on three occasions poured into the city to depose one ruler and install another. The fourth emperor has just taken power after his predecessor's suicide. Vitellius, however, is not likely to improve matters. In the words of Suetonius, his "ruling vices were extravagance and cruelty." (*The Twelve Caesars*, p. 273) He will be assassinated himself in less than a year.

Nor is the empire at peace. Threats lie along all its borders, and in the east the Jewish war has been raging for three years. It has been a vicious campaign but now it seems to be reaching its culmination. The legions of Vespasian are moving on Jerusalem. The resistance is savage, but the outcome is inevitable.

In the imperial capital it is approaching the noon hour. The sun is high in the sky and in the lower *regiones* the city is already oppressively hot. The merchants are sliding into place the panels that close up the fronts of their shops. The street stalls are cleared. The tutors have dismissed their students. Barbers have finished with their final clients. The weavers, fullers, felters, potters and the like are shutting down their work places.

On the other hand, the taverns are filling up. There are lines forming at the *tavalas caldas* as patrons pick up food to carry home. The streets, always clear of carts and animals during the day, are jammed now with people. Some are going to the baths, others to lounge in the *fora* or *basilicae*, but most are going to their homes for the midday meal and afternoon rest. Not everyone, however.

1

From different parts of the city a number of people are making their way through the maze of narrow streets and up the Aventine hill. They walk though horrific slums and near immense mansions. They pass the great temples honoring the Roman gods, their altars still running red with the blood of the day's sacrifices. Wherever two streets intersect, they encounter the small shrines dedicated to the *Lares*, who protect the neighborhood. At times, they mingle with the devotees of *Mithras* who are heading to one of their many shrines in the capital city.

Finally, singly, or in twos and threes, they enter an *insola*, one of the many apartment houses in which live the bulk of Rome's three-quarters of a million residents. Most of the apartments in these buildings are small, only two or three rooms, often barely sufficient to hold the families dwelling in them. But on the ground floor the quarters are much more commodious. Into one of these apartments the arrivals are admitted by the *janitor* (doorman).

Greeted warmly by their host, they gather in the large reception hall. Some have brought folding stools and others are seated on the couches brought in from the *triclinium* (dining room). They are a diverse group drawn from among the city's shopkeepers, artisans and merchants along with their wives and children. By their complexions, accents and, in some cases, their dress one can guess that many of the guests originally hailed from different parts of the empire. Some appear well-to-do, others are obviously not. Yet all are welcomed with equal cordiality. Though it is not the native tongue of most, the language they speak is Greek, larded now and then with a Latinism.

A simple service begins. There is singing, followed by a reading taken from the Greek translation of the Hebrew Bible. A commentary is offered. A scroll is opened containing a collection of Jesus' sayings. Some are read and more commentary is forthcoming. Members of the group have no hesitancy in offering their own views. Singing closes this part of the service.

On a small table, a loaf of bread and a cup of wine are now placed. After a brief introductory prayer, the host recounts the event that they have gathered to memorialize: "The Lord Jesus, on the night he was handed over, took bread, and, after he had given thanks, broke it and said, 'This is my body that is for you. Do this in remembrance of me.'

In the same way also the cup, after supper, saying, 'This cup is the new covenant in my blood. Do this, as often as you drink it, in remembrance of me.' For as often as you eat this bread and drink this cup, you proclaim the death of the Lord until he comes." (I Corinthians 11:23–26) The loaf of bread is broken and shared and the cup of wine is passed around. The service closes with singing.

A warm informality quickly returns as the participants open and share packets of food. Some, belonging to other groups elsewhere in the city similar to this one, bring news of their co-religionists. One or two have traveled abroad and bring reports from farther afield. To the great delight of the community, someone has brought a precious copy of a letter written by Paul of Tarsus that is now circulating among the Christian communities in the Greek provinces.

Slowly, obviously to avoid attracting undue attention, the participants slip away, hurrying down the now empty streets, returning to their shops, offices, and apartments, perhaps to get some rest before the city returns to life at midafternoon.

PREFACE

The genesis of this book lies in my reading Colleen McCullough's *The First Man in Rome* (New York: William Morrow and Company, Inc., 1990). I was struck by her vivid evocation of early Rome. Having lived in the modern city of Rome, I realized how many traces are left of the ancient one. We know more about ancient Rome than we do about any other of the urban centers from the period. We know its streets, its dwellings, its palaces and its temples. We know what its people ate and wore and how they spent their days. We know the books they read, the poetry they heard, the art they admired, the plays they enjoyed and the games they played. Not too long ago Public Television brought the viewer a gossipy re-creation of one of Rome's ruling clans.

It is generally agreed that Mark's Gospel was written in Rome or its immediate area. There is also a well-supported opinion dating the document from shortly after 70 C.E. According to Raymond Brown: "The majority of scholars date Mark in the late 60s before the destruction of the Jerusalem Temple, but the number of those who would date it after 70 is increasing." (*The Death of the Messiah*, p. 4 fnt. 1) Such being true, the writer and the readers of the first Gospel lived in the empire's capital, the city about which we know so much. My attempt, then, is to place Mark's work against the backdrop of life in ancient Rome and to see what is revealed about the Christians who created Mark's version of the "Good News."

I say "created" advisedly since the author must have reflected the religious traditions held by his fellow Christians. He would also have helped shape those traditions to meet his own readers' needs and concerns. As I tried to demonstrate in my *Exploring Scripture: How the*

5

Bible Came To Be (Mahwah, N.J.: Paulist Press, 1992), similar Christian communities lie behind all of the documents that make up the New Testament. The same is true of the Hebrew Bible[1] which reflects the traditions, concerns and needs of the people of Israel at various stages of their long history. Unfortunately for my purpose, the Scripture scholar Raymond Brown states the following: "Studies [of Mark] do not allow us to reconstruct the profile of the community addressed by Mark." (*The Churches the Apostles Left Behind*, Mahwah, N.J.: Paulist Press, 1984, p. 28) It is for this reason that Brown does not include Mark's community in his book. "While we may be able to diagnose something of Matthew's and Luke's theology by seeing how they change a source known to us [Mark], we do not have Mark's sources." (*Ibid.* pp. 28–29)

In view of what such a leading authority says, why is "a fool willing to rush in where an angel has been reluctant to tread"? A prominent Scripture scholar must walk warily, especially one whose reputation is such that his views are often taken *ex cathedra*. Others, with less formidable reputations, have more freedom. They can "push the envelope," taking the evidence to the limits of conjecture. Though such insights may be tenuous at their foundation, I believe they can, nevertheless, enrich our understanding of the first Gospel.

I wish to thank Fathers Kevin Lynch, C.S.P. and Larry Boadt, C.S.P. for their advice in preparing my manuscript. I am also grateful to Christine Nelson for her assistance and encouragement during the years that a vague idea eventually became a book.

Chapter One

THE FIRST GOSPEL

I. TRANSMITTING THE TRADITION

Communities having a low rate of literacy preserve their traditions orally. They do so in the stories they tell, in the wisdom they share and in the rituals they perform. It is something that is still done in many parts of the world today. In the early years, Christians did much the same. What they knew about Jesus' words and deeds they had heard from other Christians. Moreover, these traditions were not abstract nor were they written on stone. They were the truths members of these first Christian communities tried to live by. No tradition remains vital unless it responds to the realities of the present.

In time, written documents will play a role in preserving a community's traditions. A religious community will accept one or more written works as authoritative. These documents function as a norm which guides the community. The Koran of the Mohammedans and the writings by Joseph Smith of the Mormons function in this manner. Over many centuries, the Jews came to accept the books that make up the Hebrew Bible as norms for their religious beliefs and moral conduct. Usually, the process of acceptance is gradual. It can happen that for a period there may even be disagreement among members of a religious group as to just which are their authoritative documents.

Sometime during the fourth century B.C.E., the Hebrew Bible was translated into Greek, a work known as the Septuagint.[1] It was done to accommodate those Jews in the diaspora[2] who could no longer understand Hebrew. Many of the earliest Christians, being Jews, accepted the Septuagint as sacred Scripture. They studied these documents to find support for their belief that Jesus was the Messiah and to aid them in understanding Jesus' message. During the first century C.E. documents

7

written by Christians themselves began to circulate and were collected
by Christian communities which came to regard them as authoritative.
It was only much later that the Church itself came to an agreement on
the documents that made up what we know as the New Testament. The
earliest of these authoritative writings are those of Paul the apostle.

II. GOSPEL IN THE WRITINGS OF PAUL

A. The "Good News"

In the earliest of Paul's letters, I Thessalonians, written c. 50 C.E.,
we have: "For we know, brothers and sisters beloved by God, that he
has chosen you, because our message of the gospel came to you not in
word only, but also in power and in the Holy Spirit and with full conviction." (1:4–5) This is the earliest Christian use of the term
"Gospel."[3] It may reflect the passage from Isaiah: "The spirit of the
Lord GOD is upon me, because the LORD[4] has anointed me; he has
sent me to bring *good news* to the oppressed, to bind up the broken-
hearted, to proclaim liberty to the captives, and release to the prison-
ers." (61:1, see also 40:9; 41:27) In his letter to the Romans Paul
quotes Isaiah: "How beautiful upon the mountains are the feet of the
messenger who announces peace, who brings *good news*, who
announces salvation." (Isaiah 52:7; Romans 10:15) Paul would also
have been aware of the contemporary secular usage where the birth or
accession of a Caesar to the throne was also called "good news." For
Paul, the Gospel "is the power of God for salvation to everyone who
has faith, to the Jew first and also to the Greek." (1:15)

In many ways, Paul prepares the way for the first of the Gospels.
His career as a Christian missionary reflects that preparation.

B. The Life of Paul

Born in Tarsus, Syria, possibly around 10 C.E., Paul was a Greek-
speaking Jew, also known by his Jewish name, Saul. As he describes
himself, Paul was "circumcised on the eighth day, a member of the
people of Israel, of the tribe of Benjamin, a Hebrew born of Hebrews;
as to the law, a Pharisee; as to zeal, a persecutor of the church."
(Philippians[5] 3:5–6) He was in Jerusalem in the late 30s C.E. and par-

ticipated in an early persecution of Jesus' followers. He was sent to Damascus to arrest followers of Christ. Then, at the gates of that city, Paul underwent a conversion. (Acts 9:2ff) The story of Paul's life as a Christian missionary is told in the Acts of the Apostles.[6] The account ends with Paul's arrival in Rome c. 60 C.E.

An aspect of Paul's missionary efforts with great implications for early Christianity was his insistence that one could become a Christian without embracing Jewish ritual practices. Such a concession to the Gentile converts caused a serious disturbance among the followers of Jesus and impacted on their relationship with the Jewish communities. At one point the matter brought Paul into direct conflict with Peter, the head of the original apostles: "When Cephas came to Antioch, I opposed him to his face, because he stood self-condemned.... I said to Cephas before them all, 'If you, though a Jew, live like a Gentile and not like a Jew, how can you compel the Gentiles to live like Jews?'" (Galatians 2:11,14).

Paul was founder of several Christian communities in Asia Minor and in Greece. He also was influential in other early churches. He kept in touch with these churches by personal visits and through intermediaries. Particularly influential, however, were the letters he wrote to several of these communities. It was these letters, originating between 50 and 58 C.E., that later were accepted as authoritative by Christianity.

There is an early Christian tradition that Paul went from Rome to Spain and, on returning to the capital, was executed c. 67 C.E., possibly during the Neronian persecution. In the years that followed, Christianity continued to spread, becoming more and more a Gentile phenomenon and increasingly distinct from Judaism, its parent religion. It was most likely in these Gentile Christian communities that the heritage of Paul was preserved and where it exerted the most influence.

There is no evidence that Paul ever encountered Jesus in his lifetime. Nor did the apostle rely on those who knew Jesus: "For I want you to know, brothers and sisters, that the gospel that was proclaimed by me is not of human origin; for I did not receive it from a human source, nor was I taught it, but I received it through a revelation of Jesus Christ." (Galatians 1:11-12) We find little or no record of Jesus' words or deeds in the Pauline *corpus*. For Paul, the Gospel of Jesus is a message. In contrast, for the first evangelist, Mark, the Gospel is a story.

III. THE GOSPEL OF MARK

A. The Revolutionary Document

"Revolutionary" is an overused word. Yet, if to be revolutionary is to leave the world a different place then Mark is truly revolutionary; it is one of the most influential works ever composed. "As far as we can tell," observes Willi Marxsen, "Mark is the first to bring the individualistic element to the forming and shaping of the tradition." (*Mark the Evangelist*, p. 19) In Marxsen's view, the first evangelist presents Jesus as a living and breathing human being. The author of the first Gospel was a true innovator. He created a *genre* of sacred literature which, within fifteen or twenty years, resulted in two other Christian Gospels, those of Matthew and Luke. By the end of the century there was a fourth, that of John. In the second century, other works appeared called "gospels." None of these, however, was accepted by the Church as authoritative.

B. The Author

The writer of the first Gospel both augmented and edited the Jewish and Christian traditions he received, including those of the apostle Paul. As Paula Fredriksen observes, Mark "was not an author—he did not compose *de novo*. Nor was he a historian—he did not deal directly and critically with his evidence. The writer was an evangelist, a sort of creative editor. He organized these stories into a sequence and shaped his inherited material into something resembling a historical narrative." (*From Jesus to Christ*, pp. 3–4) In the same connection, Marxsen writes: "Here too we must consistently maintain that the work of the earliest evangelist is proclamation, that what is narrated is subordinate to it." (*Op. cit.* p. 113)

None of the earliest manuscripts of Mark's Gospel indicates the author of the document. This is true of the other Gospels as well. Authorship, important to us, was not so acute a concern for the Christian communities of the first century. Thus we have only later traditions to go by. "The earliest explicit statement about Mark as the author of a Gospel came from Papias of Hieropolis (early second century, quoted in Eusebius, HE 3.39.15); 'Mark, having become Peter's interpreter, wrote down accurately whatever he remembered of what was said or done by the Lord, however not in order.'" (*NJBC*,[7] p. 596a) There is a "Mark" referred to in other New Testament material. One "John Mark" is a companion of Paul and Barnabas. (Acts 12:12,25; 15:37,39) Paul's letters also mention a "Mark." (Colossians 4:10; II Timothy 4:11; Philemon 24) Finally, we have a reference in I Peter: "Your sister church in Babylon, chosen together with you, sends you greetings; and so does my son Mark." (5:13) It is thought that "Babylon" here is a veiled reference to "Rome." This citation then could be the source of the tradition to which Papias referred.

Yet there is a reluctance among modern Scripture scholars to accept either "John Mark" or "Mark" as the author of the first Gospel. For instance, we are told that "Mark" is from Jerusalem. (Acts 12:12,25) However, the author of Mark is very hazy on the geography of Palestine. Paul J. Achtemeier notes: "A careful scrutiny of Mark's narrative also reveals insurmountable problems for any attempt to recreate a sequentially accurate account of Jesus' career. Any attempt, for example, even to give a topographical account of Jesus' itinerary will come to grief within the Markan narrative." (*Mark*, p. 13)

As an example, we have a curious itinerary of Jesus: "Then he returned from the region of Tyre, and went by way of Sidon toward the Sea of Galilee, in the region of the Decapolis." (7:31) In fact, Sidon lies north of Tyre and the Sea of Galilee is to the south and east. Moreover, the Sea of Galilee is not really "in the region of the Decapolis." These are errors that are not likely to have been made by a well-traveled resident of the mideast. "Any attempt to straighten out this problem will again owe more to the imagination of the one who solves the problem than it will to Mark's text." (*Ibid.*)

If the author of the Gospel was a close associate of Peter and Peter is the source of his knowledge of Jesus, then our Mark is strikingly critical of the one supposed to be his mentor. The leader of the apostles is rebuked for his failure to understand Jesus' mission: "Get behind me, Satan! For you are setting your mind not on divine things but on human things." (8:31) In the garden of Gethsemani, Peter cannot stay awake. "[Jesus] came and found them sleeping; and he said to Peter, 'Simon, are you asleep? Could you not keep awake one hour?'" (14:37) Finally, it is Peter who denies Jesus three times and who is conspicuously absent at the crucifixion. One would expect a more positive presentation from a companion of the leader of the apostles.

The simple truth may be that the author of Mark chose to remain anonymous, letting his work stand on its own merits. Later, to add prestige to the Gospel, it was attributed to the known companion of both Paul and Peter. Such a conclusion in no way detracts from the merits of the first Gospel since its authoritative role stems from its acceptance by the church as part of the New Testament.

C. Place of Origin

Crucial to the understanding of any ancient document is knowing its place of origin. When we know that, we can gain some appreciation of the cultural and historical influences that affected the work's creation. Mark does contain some clues, though not many, to the locale of its composition. For instance, at one point the Gospel tells us: "A poor widow came and put in two small copper coins, which are worth a penny." (12:42) The word translated by "penny" is *quadrans*. The assumption would be that the document originated among those familiar with the *quadrans*. It is among the coinage of the western part of the empire.

We may be able to come even closer to the Gospel's point of origin. Greek was the *lingua franca* of the empire. Any document aimed at a wide readership had to be written in Greek. However, according to John P. Meier (*A Marginal Jew*, p. 326), the author of the first Gospel did not write well in that language. Raymond Brown observes: "There are more Latinisms in the Greek of Mark than in any other Gospel, and that statistic suggests a place where Latin was spoken." (*Antioch and Rome*, p. 196) The presence of Latinisms might well indicate the native tongue of the author. If so, his home would have been in *Latium*, an area which included the city of Rome and its environs.

In conclusion, we have Father Brown's observation: "The lack of a serious traditional contender favors the historicity of the second-century tradition naming Rome.... Overall, then, the internal evidence is not unfavorable to the tradition that Rome is the provenance for Mark." (*Ibid.* p. 197) The later influence of the first Gospel would have resulted, in part, from the prestige of its place of origin. Rome's status as the empire's capital was augmented for Christians by the tradition that both Peter and Paul were executed there. Our placing of Mark's creation in the empire's capital gives us a concrete background against which to examine the first Gospel. It also enables us to form some image of the Christian community for which it was written.

D. The Date of Composition

1. A ROMAN TRAGEDY

A document's date of composition supplies another aid to understanding it. Nevertheless, in ancient manuscripts, dating is frequently difficult. As noted earlier Mark was used by both Matthew and Luke as a source and thus predates them. Biblical scholars agree that these Gospels originated in the final two decades of the first century. That being the case, the 70s would seem likely for the origin of Mark. Can we be more exact?

It seems that the writing of Mark was influenced by a tragedy that had befallen a Christian community. In the Gospel Jesus warns his disciples to expect such suffering: "If any want to become my followers, let them deny themselves and take up their cross and follow me. For those who want to save their life will lose it, and those who lose their life for my sake, and for the sake of the gospel, will save it." (8:34–5) To "take up one's cross" was the equivalent of accepting a sentence of death.

In explaining the parable of the sower and the seed, Mark seems to reflect the failure of some Christians at a time of trial: "But they have no root, and endure only for a while; then, when trouble or persecution arises on account of the word immediately they fall away." (4:17) Finally, the description of events preceding the climax of history (13:9–13) could also reflect a recent persecution of a Christian community. Just such a persecution did occur in Rome.

On the night of July 18, 64 C.E., a fire broke out in the capital. By the time it had run its course a major portion of the city had been leveled with a terrible loss of life and property. In spite of Emperor Nero's efforts to alleviate the suffering of the victims, the rumor spread that he himself had the fire started to clear the way for the building of his new palace. As Tacitus, the Roman historian (c. 56–c.115 C.E.), writes: "But neither human resources, nor imperial munificence, nor appeasement of the gods eliminated sinister suspicions that the fire had been instigated. To suppress this rumor, Nero fabricated scapegoats—and punished with every refinement the notoriously depraved Christians (as they were popularly called). Their originator, Christ, had been executed in Tiberius' reign by the governor of Judea, Pontius Pilate." (*Annals*, p. 365) Here we have the first mention of Christianity's origin by a pagan author.

Tacitus states that large numbers were executed and "their deaths were made farcical. Dressed in animal skins, they were torn to pieces by dogs, or crucified, or made into torches to be ignited after dark as substitutes for daylight." (*Ibid.*) These atrocities were carried out in the imperial gardens and in the *circus* (an elliptical track for chariot racing) which Nero had built at the foot of Vatican hill.[8] Yet, "despite their guilt as Christians, and the ruthless punishment it deserved, the victims were pitied. For it was felt that they were being sacrificed to one man's brutality rather than to the national interest." (*Ibid.* p. 366) Some see in the tragedy a clue to the dating of the first Gospel. "Mark probably wrote for Roman Christians, shortly after the persecutions of Nero (64 A.D.), when the community was reeling from that tyrant's cruelty." (*The Catholic Study Bible*, p. RG 405)

However, there is a difficulty. "No other, Christian or pagan, in the following centuries refers to Nero using Christians as scapegoats, though tradition knew of Nero as a persecutor." (B.H. Warington, *Nero: Reality and Legend*, p. 125) One would expect that the events described by Tacitus would have left more of a trace in subsequent history, especially if it occasioned the writing of Mark's Gospel. It is possible that Mark's community did not suffer in the tragedy of 64 C.E. and Nero's actions were not the occasion for the composition of Mark. If so, was there another event that might have occasioned the writing of the first Gospel?

2. A JERUSALEM TRAGEDY

In 66 C.E., a revolt broke out in Palestine and the Roman military forces moved to suppress it. The battles waged on for four years and are described in considerable detail by Josephus[9] in his *The Jewish War*. The climax came in 70 C.E. when Jerusalem was captured. The city and its great temple were razed to the ground. It was an event that shocked the empire. Virtually every city had a Jewish community that would have been traumatized by what happened. Non-Jews, including Christians, were deeply moved as well.

The evangelist writing the Gospel of Luke seems to be describing the tragedy. "When you see Jerusalem surrounded by armies, then know that its desolation has come near.... they will fall by the edge of the sword and be taken away as captives among all nations; and Jerusalem will be trampled on by the Gentiles." (21:22,24) As Luke appears to reflect details of the actual event as described in *The Jewish War*, it is judged that his Gospel was written after 70 C.E.

In contrast, Mark, in the passage that parallels Luke, says only: "Do you see these great buildings? Not one stone will be left here upon another; all will be thrown down." (13:2) Some conclude that if the writer of the first Gospel had known of the temple's actual fate he would have given a more detailed account of its destruction. Those taking this view date Mark's origin before 70 C.E., usually shortly after the Neronian persecution. Nevertheless, this argument would be weakened if another plausible explanation exists.

3. AN IMPERIAL EMBARRASSMENT

The leader of the Roman forces conquering Jerusalem was Titus Flavius Vespasianus who would succeed his father, Vespasian, as emperor in 79 C.E. Josephus makes it abundantly clear that the destruction of the temple was an acute embarrassment to the future emperor. He quotes Titus as saying, "He would not make war on inanimate objects instead of men, or, whatever happened, burn down such a work of art; it was the Romans who would lose thereby, just as their empire would gain an ornament if [the temple] was preserved." (*Op. cit.* p. 356)

At the time of the disaster, Titus was absent, and in the heat of battle a Roman soldier set fire to the temple. The general himself rushed to the scene and made every effort to save the structure to no avail. As Josephus remarks: "Grief might well be bitter for the destruction of the most wonderful edifice ever seen or heard of...yet we find real comfort in the thought that Fate is inexorable, not only toward living beings, but also toward buildings and sites." (*Op. cit.* p. 359) Characteristically, Josephus carefully absolves the future emperor of blame for the tragedy.

If the first Gospel was written at the same time as *The Jewish Wars* (c. 75 C.E.) would it be surprising for Mark to be similarly circumspect? Titus would have been heir-apparent. A detailed reflection of the temple's fate in a document circulating in the capital would hardly have been politic and could have been dangerous. As will be seen later, Mark is very careful to avoid attaching any blame for the execution of Jesus to the Roman procurator, Pilate. Would he have been any less sensitive in the case of the temple's destruction by a member of the imperial family?

It is our conclusion that the Gospel of Mark appeared in Rome not long after 70 C.E. Moreover, the central theme of the work was profoundly affected by the Jerusalem tragedy. Later, in Chapter Five, we will examine in detail how the first evangelist understood the meaning of the temple's destruction. If our conclusion is correct then the first Gospel came into existence in a place and at a time about which we know a great deal—Rome in the final third of the first century C.E.

STUDY QUESTIONS

1. How did the ancient peoples preserve their religious traditions?
2. What is the Septuagint?
3. What is the origin of the term "Gospel"?
4. Who was Saul of Tarsus?
5. In what sense is the Gospel of Mark a revolutionary document?
6. What do we know of the first Gospel's author?
7. Where did the first Gospel originate?
8. What is the possible date of its composition?
9. What occurred earlier that is important to our understanding of the first Gospel?

Chapter Two

THE GRANDEUR THAT WAS ROME

I. HISTORY

By the year 69 C.E., Rome was the capital of an empire stretching from the Iberian Peninsula on the west to the border of Parthia on the east. To the south, it embraced all of North Africa and the middle east. To the north, the empire extended to the Danube, the Rhine and southern Britain. In relation to the known world of the time, Rome controlled the largest area of any empire before or since. The control over such a vast area was maintained by military power and a complex bureaucracy. The capital city was the hub of a system of highways and sea lanes rivaled only in modern times. This communication system kept money and supplies flowing into Rome. It also enabled the empire to hold in check invasions, revolts and rebellions.

At first Rome was a small city-state organized along military lines, with the male population serving as citizen-soldiers. For a long period, Rome was a republic, governed by an elected senate. The motto of the city (still used today) S.P.Q.R. means "The Senate and the People of Rome." Then, as the pre-Christian era ended, the republic was replaced by a dictatorship. Julius Caesar was assassinated to prevent his gaining dictatorial powers, but his nephew and heir Octavian assumed just such authority, taking the title, "Augustus Caesar." It was during his reign (30 B.C.E. to 14 C.E.) that Jesus of Nazareth was born.

Augustus and his successor, Tiberius (14–37 C.E.), governed with considerable skill, but the next emperor, Caligula (37–42 C.E.), was most likely insane. He was followed by Claudius (42–54 C.E.) whose

17

selection as emperor by the praetorian guard established a dangerous precedent. From this point on it was one military unit or another that deposed one ruler and installed the next. Such was the situation when Nero (54–68 C.E.), the last of the Julio-Augustan emperors, succeeded Claudius.

Nero's suicide on June 9, 68 C.E. began a period of instability and chaos. In the space of a little more than a year three army generals were proclaimed emperor, Galba, Otho and Vitellius, each ousted by the supporters of his successor. Finally, Vespasian, the first of the Flavians, came to power in December of 69 C.E. and a measure of stability returned to the empire. Of course, in the midst of all the turmoil, daily life in Rome must have gone on.

II. LIFE IN THE CAPITAL

A. *The City*

What was it like to live in Rome during the last third of the first century? Forget those opulent Roman backgrounds from the movies with their scenes of broad avenues where chariots and carts jostle for passage past luxurious mansions. Only the few very rich could occupy a single family dwelling. Shopkeepers usually lived over their place of business. Most of Rome's three quarters of a million inhabitants lived in a crowded warren of narrow streets and high-rise apartment buildings (*insulae*). Some of these had as many as nine floors. There were few amenities. Indoor plumbing, save for the ground floor, did not exist. Shutters alone closed the windows. For heating and cooking there were only small charcoal braziers.

Nevertheless, not all the *insulae* were occupied by the poor. The moderately well off might take up residence in one. Julius Caesar's first home was the ground floor of an *insula*. Like the future emperor, most of those of modest means lived in the better quarters of an apartment house. The poor of the city, and there were many, crowded in wherever they could. Privacy was a privilege only of the well-to-do in the capital city.

There was one blessing. During the day, no cart, no wheeled vehicle, could enter the city. People, in many ways, lived in the streets, narrow as they were. The barbers cared for their clients, the tutors taught their classes and scribes read or penned letters. In stalls, produce, fresh from the countryside, was sold. From the shops that lined the street every manner of need was met, bread, fish, wine and prepared foods, hot and cold. There were bakers, launderers, tailors and shoemakers. Some neighborhoods specialized in particular trades. The carpenters and potters here, there the fullers (they got things white) and there the felters (who made hats and heavy cloaks).

"It is clear, however, that even in the little alleys a vibrant sense of community joined the inhabitants, leaning on their window-sills to see the sights and talk with each other from apartment to apartment, while, lacking room at home, the flayer below stripped the hide off a carcass on the sidewalk, the teacher taught his circle of pupils their ABC's, the notary or scribe drew up a rental contract at his table, the barber shaved his customers, the cloth cleaner hung garments out to dry, the butcher cut up meat." (Ramsey MacMullen, *Roman Social Relations*, pp. 63–64) In fact, Mark's Rome appeared not all that different from the tenement area of an American city in the last century.

We don't want to paint too grim a picture. The two hundred and fifty miles of the city's viaducts were a magnificent architectural and engineering achievement. From them an ample supply of fresh water came into the city and flowed to the fountains in each *regione*. The farms, gardens and vineyards surrounding the city usually supplied plentiful amounts of vegetables, dairy products and wine. In times of food shortages, moreover, the government and private sources imported inexpensive or even free wheat for the inhabitants.

The forums, law courts (*basilicae*), temples and public gardens gave the population spacious areas in which to gather. Finally, there were the public baths, combination spas, health clubs and libraries open to the Romans for a modest fee. Their extensive ruins, visible in all parts of modern Rome, give us striking evidence of the city's former glory. As MacMullen observes, "We can assert as certain that the bulk of the population [of Rome] had typically to put up with the most uncomfortable crowding at home, made tolerable by the attractive spaciousness of public facilities." (*Ibid.* p. 63)

B. The Inhabitants

"As a consequence of Rome's entry into the East and her active interest in the cities, urban society became somewhat more complex than it had been even during the Hellenistic age. For a very long time groups of foreigners had gathered in each city: merchants and artisans following the armies or in search of better markets or better access to transportation, persons enslaved and displaced by war or piracy and now set free, political exiles, soldiers of fortune." (Wayne A. Meeks, *The First Urban Christians*, p. 13) These non-citizen residents were known as *metoikoi* and nowhere would their presence be more in evidence than in the empire's capital. A Roman forum was a kaleidoscope of languages and native dress. All went to make up a very cosmopolitan city that was literally the crossroads of the world.

Roman society was sharply pyramidal. At the pinnacle were the emperor and a small elite of the wealthy. Jérôme Carcopino paints a grim picture:

> There was nothing between the satellite plutocracy of the court and the mass of plebes too poor to exist without the doles of an emperor and the charity of the rich.... Directly or indirectly then, at least one-third, and possibly one-half of the population of the city lived on public charity.... The numerical inferiority of the Haves to the horde of the Have-Nots, sufficiently distressing in itself, becomes positively terrifying when we realize the inequality of fortune within the minority; the majority of what we should nowadays call the middle class vegetated in semistarvation within sight of the almost incredible opulence of a few thousand multimillionaires. (*Daily Life in Ancient Rome*, pp. 65–66)

Only Roman citizens could play a role in the public life of the capital. Some possessed this prerogative from birth, others received it by concession.[1] As a rule the citizen of Rome did not work. "The truth is that there were very few professions open to the gentleman in Rome." (R. W. Moore, *The Roman Commonwealth*, p. 91) In fact, having to work for a living was looked down upon as we can see from Cicero: "The profession of a worker for wages is a low calling.... Every industrial worker follows a sordid calling." (quoted *ibid.* p. 97) Most indigent Romans took advantage of the patronage system. By being of assistance as needed, the citizen received from his wealthy patron a modest income and could spend his days at leisure. The non-citizens living in the capital struggled along as best they could.

The old saw that the emperor kept a restive population quiet by supplying "bread and circuses" is not far from the truth. The bulk of Rome's citizenry was kept preoccupied by a steady supply of public entertainment. The Circus Maximus held a quarter of a million spectators. In addition there were lesser race courses, numerous theaters and amphitheaters. At one point a seat at some form of amusement existed for every citizen residing in the city. Tragically, much of that entertainment was the bloody combat between men and beasts. "[The Romans] also had a rich capacity for enjoyment, in music and the spoken word, theaters, buildings and athletics. Their enjoyment could also involve great violence, in the gladiatorial shows and the pitting of wild beasts against the city's convicted criminals." (Robin Lane Fox, *Pagans and Christians*, p. 57)

C. A Slave Society

For all their poverty, the poor of Rome did have one advantage; they were free. Many others were not as fortunate. According to Michael Grant, "At Rome, out of about one million inhabitants, perhaps a quarter were slaves. Many of them came from Europe, many more from Asia Minor and Syria, and perhaps one-eighth from outside the empire." (*The World of Rome*, p. 132) Many of these slaves were from conquered populations. Others had been sold into slavery as the result of debt or crime. Still others were simply the children of slaves.

Another source of slaves came from a grisly aspect of Roman life: "… until the beginning of the third century…[the *pater familias*] might expose his new-born child to perish of cold and hunger or be devoured by dogs on one of the public refuse dumps, unless rescued by the pity of some passerby." (Carcopino, op. cit. p. 77) Not all passersby were motivated by pity. Such a child could be raised and sold as a slave.

The number of slaves in a household might range from hundreds to only one or two. They did most of the city's menial labor. As a result there was no class of wage-earning employees in Rome. The slave was completely at the mercy of the master who could dispose of the slave as he saw fit. Some owners would set a slave free (*manumission*). Still, a manumitted slave remained under some obligation to his former master and even to his heirs. Among the better off and even the well-to-do of the city were ex-slaves. "Former slaves also became doctors, jurists, school teachers, artisans, shopkeepers, bailiffs, jockeys, auctioneers, copyists, dancers, and pimps." (Grant, *op. cit.* p. 119)

It is in Rome, then, with its polyglot population, a mixture of native-born and immigrant, few rich and many poor, slave and free, that we find the Christians for whom Mark wrote his Gospel. They were part of the panoply of religions found in the empire's capital during the first century C.E. In fact, few locales in history show us a more varied assembly of religious beliefs.

III. PRE-CHRISTIAN RELIGIONS IN ROME

A. *The Cult of the State*

In his work, *The Ancient City*, Numa Denis Fustel de Coulanges tells the reader:

> We must inquire what place religion occupied in the life of a Roman. His house was for him what a temple is for us. He finds there his worship and his gods. His fire is a god; the walls, the doors, the threshhold are gods; the boundary marks which surround his field are also gods. The tomb is an altar, and his ancestors are divine beings.
>
> Each one of his daily actions is a rite; his whole day belongs to his religion. Morning and evening he invokes his fire, his Penates, and his ancestors; in leaving and entering his house he addresses a prayer to them. Every meal is a religious act, which he shares with his domestic divinities. Birth, initiation, the taking of the toga, marriage, and the anniversaries of all these events, are the solemn acts of his worship....
>
> Every day he sacrifices in his house, every month in his cury, several months a year with his gens or his tribe. Above all these gods, he must offer worship to those of the city. There are in Rome more gods than citizens.
>
> He offers sacrifices to thank the gods; he offers them, and by far the greater number, to appease their wrath. One day he figures in a procession, dancing after a certain ancient rhythm, to the sound of the sacred flute. Another day he conducts chariots, in which lie statues of the divinities. Another time it is a lectisternium: a table is set in a street,

and loaded with provisions, upon beds lie statues of the gods, and every Roman passes bowing, with a crown upon his head, and a branch of laurel in his hand.... This Roman whom we present here is not the man of the people, the feeble-minded man whom misery and ignorance have made superstitious. We are speaking of the patrician, the noble, powerful, and rich man. (pp. 211, 212)

Every aspect of life in first century Rome was saturated with religion. Shrines to the household gods, the *penates,* were found in every home. In the courtyard of each apartment house and at every street corner were shrines to the *lares,* spirits protecting the local area. Similarly protecting spirits were honored by every social group, activity and even the nation itself. To these were added the Roman pantheon, gods and goddesses mostly borrowed from the Greeks. In their honor were erected the magnificent temples that graced every part of the city. Few moments in the daily life of the Roman were free of religious reminders.

As with all ancient cultures, religion had played a central role in the history of the city and the empire. Emperor Augustus had attempted to restore the state religion to its former glory by repairing older temples and building new ones to honor the gods. He financed priesthoods to care for these buildings and to carry out the sacred rituals. He also insisted on public participation in the ceremonies. He did this not simply for reasons of piety but to strengthen the role of the emperor. Augustus was faced with the task of unifying the empire after the civil wars that had preceded his coming to power. "Thus the Augustan age is the classic age of Roman religion. In it the canons of religious observance were laid down once and for all and an official State religion came into being." (Moore, *op. cit.* p. 103) His efforts were augmented by the divinization of the emperors themselves.

In the long run, however, the efforts of Augustus failed. The state-sanctioned cults had lost their hold on the people. Carcopino observes:

The Roman pantheon still persisted, apparently immutable; the ceremonies which had for centuries been performed on the dates prescribed by the pontiffs from their sacred calendars continued to be carried out in accordance with the ancestral custom. But the spirits of men had fled from the old religion; it still commanded their service but no longer their hearts or their belief. With its indeterminate gods and its colorless myths, mere fables concocted from details suggested by Latin topography or pale reflections of the adventures which had overtaken the Olympians of Greek epic; with its prayers formulated in the style of legal contracts and as dry as the procedure of a lawsuit; with its lack of metaphysical curiosity and indifference to moral value; with the narrow-minded banality of its field of action, limited to the interests of the city and the development of practical politics—Roman religion froze the impulses of faith by its coldness and its prosaic utilitarianism. It sufficed at the most to reassure the soldier against the risks of war or a peasant against the rigors of unseasonable weather, but in the motley Rome of the second century it had wholly lost its power over the human heart. (*Op. cit.* pp. 121–122)

As we come to the period of our concern another blow had been given to the state-sponsored cults. "Even the enthusiasm which the imperial cult had awakened at the outset had in turn gone cold; it was now nothing more than another cog in the great official machine which functioned in virtue of its acquired momentum but had long since lost its soul. The fall of Nero and the extinction with him of the family of Augustus had dealt a fatal blow by depriving the worship of the emperors of its dynastic sanctity." (*Ibid.* pp. 125–126) As the hold of the official religion of the state over the population weakened, a dramatic change took place.

B. The Mystery Religions

Into the spiritual vacuum left by the fading official cults flowed the mystery religions of the eastern regions of the empire and from Egypt. These new religions came with the immigrants to the city. "These non-citizen residents, or metics (*metoikoi*), often retained some sense of ethnic identity by establishing local cults or their native gods...." (Meeks, *op. cit.* p. 13) Carcopino sums up the change:

Faith, however, had not entirely disappeared from Rome. Far from it. It had not even diminished.... faith had extended its domain and increased in intensity. Roman faith had merely changed its object and direction. It had turned away from the official polytheism and taken refuge in the "chapels" now formed by the philosophic sects and by the brotherhoods that celebrated the mysteries of the Oriental gods. Here believers could at last find an answer to their questionings and a truce to their anxieties; here were at once an explanation of the world, rules of conduct, release from evil and from death.... we observe a paradox that Rome has begun to possess a religious life, in the sense in which we understand the word today, at the very moment when her State religion has ceased to live in men's consciences. (*Ibid.* p. 128)

These cults were called mystery religions because of a common feature. When initiated into one of these cults, the newcomer received secret information. This "wisdom" purported to assure personal salvation. "More importantly, most of these eastern religions had a central myth which explored the death and resurrection of a deity or a figure closely associated with a deity. This victory over death served as a promise to the adherents that they, too, could achieve immortality and a blessed life after death. Assurance of an afterlife could be granted, however, only to people who had been initiated into the mysteries of the religion." (Jo-Ann Shelton, *As Romans Did*, pp. 394–395)

One of the earliest to arrive from the east was Cybele, the "Great Mother" whom her cult members honored along with her consort, Attis. The latter, who rose from the dead, was a symbol of immortality. Another early cult was that of Dionysus, the Greek god of fertility, who also was said to have conquered death. Very popular too was the worship of the Egyptian diety, Isis, whose consort, Osiris, like Attis and Dionysus, had been killed and had risen again.

A late arrival (first century B.C.E.) from Asia Minor was the cult of Mithras. "Mithras was again and again the go-between for men, their great helper in the fight with evil which he will finally destroy at his second coming." (Carl Christ, *The Romans*, p. 164) The cult's ceremonies included a baptism in the blood of a slain bull and a dedicatory meal of bread and water. As Carl Christ notes: "At all events, it was 'Mithraism' and not the ancient Greco-Roman pantheon or the emperor cult which became the most important antithesis to Christianity." (*Ibid.*) The followers of Mithras were growing in number at the same time as Christianity spread. "During these first two centuries C.E. the cult of Mithras was spreading very widely indeed throughout the west. Rome, as a great cosmopolitan city, was a natural place for its development; we know of forty-five *Mithraea* in the city and its suburbs."

(Grant, *op. cit.* p. 203) The appeal of the two religions, nevertheless, differed on an important point. Only males, usually soldiers, could be members of Mithraic communities.

Joining a mystery cult did not mean forsaking the state religious ceremonies and rituals. Emperor Nero is said to have been a devotee of Isis. Official religious rituals remained a part of social and civic life. Their public religious duties being fulfilled, the residents of Rome were free to pay homage to whatever other deities they chose. These were worshiped in magnificent temples, in small shrines (as in the case of Mithras) or in private homes.

C. The Jews

One group refused to pay any homage to any God other than its own. Jews had been present in the capital city since the middle of the second century B.C.E. Their exclusiveness was a constant source of tension. The government did grant the Jews certain privileges, exempting them from participation in the rituals of the official religion. Yet, these grants could be and were revoked at times.

The life of the Jew in Rome was not an easy one, though some did rise to positions of wealth and power. Tiberius took severe measures against them, shipping four thousand of Rome's Jews to Sardinia. Claudius banished the whole group from the city. About the same time the poet and satirist, Juvenal, mocked the Jews with the following lines:

> Those whose lot it was that their fathers worshipped the Sabbath
> Pray to nothing now but the clouds and a spirit in Heaven;
> Since their father abstained from pork, they'd be cannibals sooner
> Than violate that taboo. Circumcised, not as the Gentiles,
> They despise Roman law, but learn and observe and revere
> Israel's code, and all from the sacred volume of Moses ...
> *Remember the Sabbath Day, to keep it lazy...(Satires,* p. 164*)*

Christianity came to Rome amid the city's Jews and remained a part of that community for some time. During this period, Christians enjoyed the exemptions that had been granted to the Jews. Like them the early Christians were not required to participate in state-mandated religious rituals. In time, clashes over accepting Jesus as the Messiah and over circumcision and the dietary restrictions soon alienated the two communities from each other. The parting was far from amicable, especially as Christians, now no longer enjoying the Jewish exemptions, were exposed to persecution.

STUDY QUESTIONS

1. Who was the Emperor of Rome in 70 C.E.?
2. In the first century C.E., what did life in Rome resemble?
3. Who were the *metoikoi*?
4. What were the *penates* and the *lares*?
5. What were the "mystery religions"?
6. What important cult was contemporary with Christianity?
7. What crucial privilege was granted to the Jews by Roman rulers?

Chapter Three

CHRISTIANITY IN ROME

I. EARLY HISTORY

A. The Arrival

Christianity came to the empire's capital very early on. Suetonius, the Roman historian (c. 69–c. 140 C.E.), wrote, "Because the Jews at Rome caused continuous disturbances at the instigation of Chrestus, [Claudius] expelled them from the city." (*The Twelve Caesars*, p. 202) As *Chrestus* is most likely a variant of the Latin *Christus*, the dispute that caused the ruckus was apparently between those Jews who accepted Jesus as the Messiah and those who didn't. Paul's letters and the Acts of the Apostles give ample testimony to such disputes among the Jews. We have a reference to the expulsion in the book of Acts: "Paul left Athens and went to Corinth. There he found a Jew named Aquila, a native of Pontus, who had recently come from Italy with his wife Priscilla, because Claudius had ordered all Jews to leave Rome." (18:2) Later, we will see more of Aquila and his wife.

As Claudius ruled from 42 to 54 C.E., the first followers of Jesus must have arrived in Rome some time during the 40s, within ten years of Jesus' execution. We saw that the Jewish community in the capital was long established and of considerable prestige. These first Christians,[1] themselves Jews, would naturally have gravitated toward their fellow countrymen. They must have soon won adherents among the Jews in Rome. Later, this must have given rise to the unrest leading to the emperor's decree of expulsion mentioned above.

B. Paul Comes to Rome

In 58 C.E. Paul the apostle wrote from Corinth, "Paul, a servant of Jesus Christ, called to be an apostle.... To all God's beloved in

28

Rome...." (Romans 1:1,7) Paul has not as yet visited the capital but the lengthy list of acquaintances he greets at the close of the letter (16:1–15) indicates that he had knowledge of the Christians living there. The letter is written to a community of both Jews and Gentiles. The latter predominate, but the Jewish traditions are still held in esteem. Paul reflects such respect in his praise of Abraham: "No distrust made him waver concerning the promise of God, but he grew strong in his faith as he gave glory to God...." (4:20) In addition the apostle speaks of "our ancestor Isaac." (9:10)

Paul also mutes his criticism of Jewish customs, stressing tolerance of differing practices. "Some judge one day to be better than another, while others judge all days to be alike. Let all be fully convinced in their own minds. Those who observe the day, observe it in honor of the Lord. Also those who eat, eat in honor of the Lord, since they give thanks to God; while those who abstain, abstain in honor of the Lord and give thanks to God." (14:5–6) Here Paul is more diplomatic than he was in writing to the Galatians. In that letter, speaking of those who were insisting that Christians must be circumcised, Paul said, "I wish those who unsettle you would castrate themselves!" (5:12)

Though he is tolerant of those who still observe the Jewish rituals, Paul makes clear that the Gentile converts are free of such restrictions: "But now we are discharged from the law...so that we are slaves not under the old written code but in the new life of the Spirit." (7:6) What unites Jew and Gentile is faith, "since God is one; and he will justify the circumcised on the ground of faith and the uncircumcised through that same faith." (3:30) However, there was doubtless tension between those holding to these two differing traditions.

Three years after writing the letter, Paul himself arrives in Rome (Acts 28:14–16) and is greeted by the Christian leaders. Though under house arrest, "[Paul] lived there two whole years at his own expense and welcomed all who came to him, proclaiming the kingdom of God and teaching about the Lord Jesus Christ with all boldness and without hindrance." (Acts 28:31–32) We do not know how long Paul remained in the capital city. As noted earlier, tradition has it that he left Rome, but later returned and was executed.

We have no further knowledge of the Christians associated with

Paul in Rome. We have noted the report of Tacitus (*op. cit.* pp. 365–366) that Christians were persecuted during the reign of Nero around 64 C.E., but we have no way of knowing just how they might have been related to the community Paul addressed. It is not until some ten years later, with the appearance of Mark's Gospel, that we have our next evidence of a Christian presence in the empire's capital.

II. THE CHURCHES OF ROME

A. Ekklesia *in Paul*

How would a Christian community have appeared in the last quarter of the current era's first century? Most of what we know must be gleaned from the authentic letters of Paul,[2] the assumption being that the patterns found in his communities would have been reflected in the other Christian communities of the empire. Local variations, of course, would have been present.

In the earliest of his letters, Paul writes, "To the church of the Thessalonians in God the Father and the Lord Jesus Christ." (I Thessalonians 1:1) We have a similar greeting when he writes to the Corinthians, "To the church of God that is in Corinth." (I Corinthians 1:2; II Corinthians 1:1) In English translations "church"[3] is used for the Greek *ek-klesia*. In Hellenistic culture the word referred to a civil assembly meeting for legislative or deliberative purposes.

In the Septuagint, the Greek translation of the Hebrew Bible, *ek-klesia* translates the Hebrew word *kahal*. Among the Jews of Paul's time the *kahal Yahweh*, the "assembly of God," designated those Jewish communities located outside of Jerusalem. Paul took over the term and used it to designate a local Christian community over thirty times. The use of the term "church" to designate Christianity as a whole does not appear until it is found in Colossians and Ephesians, letters attributed to Paul but written later in the first century C.E.

Given the frequency of the *ekklesia* in the Pauline corpus, over sixty times, its absence in the Gospels of Mark, Luke and John is surprising. Matthew uses the term on but three occasions. It may be that the evangelists were aware that the term only came into use after the death and resurrection of Jesus.

B. *The House Church*

The question arises, in what sort of places did these early Christians gather together? We read in the Acts of the Apostles, "Day by day, as [Christians] spent much time together in the temple, they broke bread[4] at home...." (2:46) The early custom of Christians meeting in homes while remaining practicing Jews must have continued for some time. They could participate in the services of the synagogues and gather separately in the home of a fellow believer. However, with the expansion of the Gentile mission under Paul and others, Christian communities were more frequently on their own.

Writing to the church in Corinth from Ephesus, the apostle concludes, "The churches of Asia send greetings. Aquila and Prisca, together with the church in their house, greet you warmly in the Lord." (I Corinthians 16:19) Later, in his letter to Rome Paul includes, "Greet Prisca and Aquila....Greet also the church in their house." (Romans 16:3,5) In pleading the cause of Onesimus, a fugitive slave, Paul writes to Philemon and sends greetings "to the church in your house." (Philemon 2) Finally, in a letter attributed to Paul we have, "Give my greetings to the brothers and sisters in Laodicea, and to Nympha and the church in her house." (Colossians 4:15) The custom of meeting in private homes appears to have become the general practice.

"Our sources," writes Meeks, "give us good reason to think that [the individual household] was the basic unit in the establishment of Christianity in the city...." (*Op. cit.* p. 29) Further, he notes, "... the household was much broader than the family in Western societies, including not only immediate relatives but also slave, freedmen, hired workers, and sometimes tenants and partners in trade or craft.... new converts would have certainly been added to existing household communities." (*Ibid.* pp. 75–76) It is possible that such close-knit families all became converts to Christianity together. Paul cites an example: "Now, brothers and sisters, you know that members of the household of Stephanas were the first converts in Achaia." (I Corinthians 16:15)

There is a hint of the house church in John's Gospel. At the last supper when Jesus has just announced that one of those present would betray him, we read: "One of his disciples—the one whom Jesus loved—was reclining next to [Jesus]; Simon Peter therefore motioned to him to ask Jesus of whom he was speaking. So while reclining next to Jesus, he asked him, 'Lord, who is it?'" (13:23–25) This exchange makes perfect sense if the three are lying side-by-side on a *triclinium*[5] with Jesus in the center. Jesus and "the one whom Jesus loved" are facing each other with Jesus' back to Peter. John pictured Jesus and his companions dining in the manner in which the evangelist himself may have dined in a house church.

C. The Local Church

Most Christians, like their fellow urbanites in the other cities of the empire, lived in small apartments. Such restricted living quarters would have limited a house church to membership of only a dozen or so. Yet Paul at times addresses what seems to be a larger gathering: "If, therefore, the whole church comes together...." (I Corinthians 14:23) "Gaius, who is host to me and to the whole church, greets you." (Romans 16:23) Particularly telling is Paul's reference to the "Lord's supper" in I Corinthians (11:20–22). What he describes does not appear to be an intimate gathering of a family and a few outsiders. It is a larger group, some of whom appear to be strangers to one another.

Vincent Branick in his book, *The House Church in the Writings of Paul*, notes, "The private dwelling functioned for the church on two levels. It formed the environment for house churches strictly speaking, gatherings of Christians around one family in the house of that family.... On a second broader level, the private dwelling formed the environment for gatherings of the local church, the assembly of all the Christian households and individuals of a city." (pp. 13–14) Paul makes mention of individual house churches. However, his authentic letters, with the exception of Philemon, are addressed to the Christians of a city or, as in the case of Galatians, a group of cities: "To the church of the Thessalonians in God the Father and the Lord Jesus Christ" (I Thessalonians 1:1), "To the churches of Galatia" (Galatians 1:2), "To the church of God that is in Corinth" (I Corinthians 1:2; II Corinthians 1:1), "To all the saints in Christ Jesus who are in Philippi" (Philippians 1:1), "To all God's beloved in Rome" (Romans 1:7). We can assume that there was a local church in each of these cities; perhaps there were more than one.

"For about a century, the private dwelling shaped the Christians' community life, forming the environment in which Christians related to each other, providing an economic substructure for the community, a platform for missionary work, a framework for leadership and authority, and probably a definite role for women." (Branick, *op. cit.* pp. 13–14) Apparently, in the second century C.E., the house church involving one family and associates is gradually replaced by the local church meeting in a building totally dedicated to religious purposes, though apparently it kept the name of the family that had donated the building.[6] For the next two centuries and a half Christianity will not be a legally authorized religion and will be frequently the object of persecution. As a result, its adherents will not be able to worship publicly. So, until the Edict of Toleration issued under Constantine in 312 C.E., the local churches, as a rule, met in such converted dwellings.

D. House Churches in Rome

1. SANTA PRISCA

The apostle Paul may have had a particularly close relationship with one of Rome's house churches. In the letter to the Romans, Paul singles out two old friends. "Greet Prisca and Aquila, who work with me in Christ Jesus, and who risked their necks for my life." (16:3–4) Prisca and Aquila were first generation believers, having been among the Jewish Christians expelled from the city by Claudius. They went to Corinth where Paul met them in 51 C.E. "There [Paul] found a Jew named Aquila, a native of Pontus, who had recently come from Italy with his wife Priscilla [Prisca to the Romans], because Claudius had ordered all Jews to leave Rome. Paul went to see them, and, because he was of the same trade, he stayed with them, and they worked together—by trade they were tentmakers." (Acts 18:2–3) The vision of Paul and his two new friends sitting together and speaking of Christ as they stitched together the heavy tent-cloth is an endearing one.

Paul remained in Corinth for a year and a half before he sailed to Ephesus, taking Priscilla and Aquila with him. (Acts 18:18–19) When Paul moved on in 52 C.E. his friends remained in Ephesus. We can assume that they worked with the Christian community the apostle left behind. We know that when Paul returned to Ephesus his friends were still there since in a letter written to Corinth in 57 C.E. Paul says, "Aquila and Prisca...greet you warmly in the Lord." (I Corinthians 16:19) However, when Paul wrote to Rome from Corinth in the following year, his friends must have already returned to the capital, being there when his letter arrived.

The final verses of the Acts of the Apostles are: "[Paul] lived there two whole years at his own expense and welcomed all who came to him, proclaiming the kingdom of God and teaching about the Lord Jesus Christ with all boldness and without hindrance." (28:30–31) Is it too great a leap of imagination to say that between 61 and 63 C.E. Paul lived in Rome with his two old friends and companions, Prisca and Aquila? To take a further leap, could not this most prestigious house church have survived another ten years, bringing it into the time of Mark's Gospel?

It is interesting to note that on Rome's Aventine hill today, there are the remains of a fourth century church honoring St. Prisca. It is said to have been erected on the site of her and Aquila's home. As these fourth century churches in Rome were frequently built on the sites of house churches we can assume that such was true of St. Prisca's. In fact, the first twenty-five Christian structures built in Rome, dating from the fourth century, appear to have been built on sites of such house churches.[7]

2. SAN CLEMENTE

Further insights into house churches can be gained from archeological findings beneath the Roman church of San Clemente. The present structure dates from the middle ages. In the mid-1800s, excavations revealed the remains of an earlier fourth century Christian church. It was built just after Constantine gave Christianity legal standing and freed its members from the threat of persecution. Further excavations were made at a deeper level early in this century. These brought to light two additional structures dating from the first century C.E. They were built upon the debris left by the fire that had destroyed the area during the reign of Emperor Nero.

One of these buildings contains the remains of a Mithraic shrine and associated facilities, possibly a dining hall and a classroom. Across a narrow passageway are the vestiges of another structure. It also lies directly below San Clemente and appears to have been a large residence. Belonging to the Clementine family, it was also the site of a house church.[8] A member of that family may be the author of the early Christian document, *The First Letter of Clement of Rome.* It may possibly be that at some point, the Clementine home became the site of one of Rome's local churches.

It is not difficult to imagine the adherents of Mithras making their way quite openly to one of the many *Mithrea* of the capital. In that narrow passageway they would have mingled with the followers of Jesus. These Christians would have had to be quite circumspect as to their destination. A *Mithraeum* also lies below the church dedicated to St. Prisca on the Aventine. We are reminded again that in these first centuries the mystery religion involving the worship of Mithras was Christianity's chief rival.

In the Prologue, I have given an imaginary evocation of what a Christian meeting in a house church might have been like in the early years. How differently things would appear three centuries later when the first Christian church structures[9] were built. Who would have guessed in the 70s C.E. that one day it would not be temples or shrines honoring the gods and god-like emperors that rose above the landscape of Rome? Yet, in a few centuries, the skyline would be dotted with buildings dedicated to the worship of the Nazorean.

III. CHURCH RITUALS

A. The Gatherings

Meeks reminds us how different Christian churches were from the other religious communities of their day: "Not only did the first-century Christians lack shrines, temples, cult statues, and sacrifices; they stage no public festivals, dances, musical performances, pilgrimages, and as far as we know they set up no inscriptions." (*Op. cit.* p. 140) Yet they could not have been devoid of what is essential to any religion and that is ritual. As Meeks defines it, "Ritual is often said to be symbolic action, representing what the society holds to be of primary importance, or indeed the very structure of society." (*Op. cit.* p. 141) Unfortunately, Mark gives us little evidence of early Christian ritual.

However, we can assume that Mark's community would have reflected to some degree what we learn from Paul's letters. The apostle, in connection with his discussion of the Lord's supper, speaks of "coming together." (I Corinthians 11:17,18,20,33,34) These must have been regular gatherings of the local churches and possibly of the house churches as well. Besides the Lord's supper which we will return to shortly, we can only conjecture as to what other rituals may have been involved in these meetings. Paul gives us a hint: "When you come together, each one has a hymn, a lesson, a revelation, a tongue,[10] or an interpretation." (14:26) Singing, reading from Scripture, commentary on what was read and the like must have characterized the gatherings of the Pauline communities. Mark's community no doubt gathered to celebrate in a similar manner.

B. Baptism

We can probably make the same assumption with baptism. This was undoubtedly the initiation rite characteristic of the Christians. Its importance can be seen in Paul: "As many of you as were baptized into Christ have clothed yourselves with Christ" (Galatians 3:27), "For in the one Spirit we were all baptized into one body—Jews or Greeks, slaves or free—and we were all made to drink of one Spirit" (I Corinthians 12:13), "Do you not know that all of us who have been baptized into Christ Jesus were baptized into his death?" (Romans 6:3)

Mark makes no specific reference to such a ritual. He makes mention only of the baptism of Jesus by John which was not an initiation rite but a symbol of repentance (1:4). What is likely is that Mark did not have a tradition of either Jesus or his disciples baptizing. However, given the role of baptism in Paul, it does not seem possible that the ceremony had no place in Mark's church.

In this connection we can make another supposition. As noted above, the local church most likely had the use of a larger home for its gatherings. These homes frequently had a small catch basin (*impluvium*) in the entrance hall (*atrium*) or more elaborate pool in the building's courtyard (*peristylium*). Given their need of privacy, we can conclude that it was in one or the other of these that Mark's Christians were baptized.

C. *The Lord's Supper*

1. THE TRADITIONS

As noted above, the focus of regular Christian gatherings was "the Lord's supper." (I Corinthians 11:20) From Paul, we learn that this ritual was accompanied by a sort of "pot-luck" supper which in the case of Corinth was the subject of some abuses. (11:18–22) In the course of admonishing the community, Paul recounts the institution of the ritual by Jesus. The passage most likely reflects the ritual formula used by the community:

> For I received from the Lord what I also handed on to you, that the Lord Jesus on the night when he was betrayed took a loaf of bread, and when he had given thanks, he broke it and said, "This is my body that is for you. Do this in remembrance of me." In the same way he took the cup also, after supper, saying, "This cup is the new covenant in my blood. Do this, as often as you drink it, in remembrance of me." For as often as you eat this bread and drink the cup, you proclaim the Lord's death until he comes. (11:23–26)

Meals taken in common by a community are an almost universal expression of group unity. The Passover meal of the Jews comes immediately to mind and may be the origin of the "Lord's supper." Similar meals were found in the pagan worship of the period as well. Such a theme of unity is found in Paul: "The cup of blessing that we bless, is it not a sharing in the blood of Christ? The bread that we break, is it not a sharing in the body of Christ? Because there is one bread, we who are many are one body, for we all partake of the one bread." (10:16–17)

2. IN MARK

Though we have no direct evidence of the "Lord's supper" in Mark, again we can assume it was celebrated in his churches as well. In the first Gospel's account of Jesus' last meal with his disciples we may have the formula used by Mark's community: "While they were eating, he took a loaf of bread, and after blessing it he broke it, gave it to them, and said, 'Take; this is my body.' Then he took a cup, and after giving thanks he gave it to them, and all of them drank from it. He said to them, 'This is my blood of the covenant, which is poured out for many.'" (14:22–24) It is a different ritual formula from the one we saw above in Paul.

In groups small and sometimes large, the Christians reflected in Mark's Gospel gathered to hear the word and share the meal that expressed their unity. They echoed what Paul said of the Christians in Corinth: "The cup of blessing that we bless, is it not a sharing in the blood of Christ? The bread that we break, is it not a sharing in the body of Christ? Because there is one bread, we who are many are one body, for we all partake of the one bread." (I Corinthians 10:16–17)

There was a difference. Mark's Christians added the following, having Jesus say: "Truly I tell you, I will never again drink of the fruit of the vine until that day when I drink it new in the kingdom of God." (14:25) Their celebration of the Lord's supper may have served as a reminder to these Christians that in a short time they would be joining Jesus in that kingdom and sharing with him the "new" wine. Later we will see more of this expectation which characterized Mark's communities.

STUDY QUESTIONS

1. When do we have the earliest trace of Christianity in Rome?
2. What does the Letter to the Romans tell us about a Christian community in the empire's capital?
3. When did Paul visit Rome?
4. What Hebrew word does the Greek *ek-klesia* translate?
5. What was a house church?
6. Who were some of those who had Christian communities meeting in their homes?
7. What was a local church?
8. What do present-day Rome's Santa Prisca and San Clemente have in common?
9. What early church rituals would have taken place in the house and local churches?
10. What was the "Lord's Supper"?

Chapter Four

MARK'S CHRISTIANS

I. INTRODUCTION

Who were the people who gathered in the house churches and came together in the local church that made up the Christian community behind Mark's Gospel? They must have been drawn from the urban population typical of the empire's cities. Though each of these cities had individual characteristics, the urban centers of the first century of the current era were a combination of local and foreign populations, something particularly true of Rome. Granting that there were similarities between cities, we can get a clearer picture of the members of Mark's churches from what we see in Paul's letters.

II. THE PAULINE CHRISTIANS

A. The Entrepreneurs

In describing the "first urban Christians" that made up the Pauline communities, Meeks writes: "It is a picture in which several social levels are brought together. The extreme top and bottom of the Greco–Roman social scale are missing." (*Op. cit.* p. 73) As the bulk of the population was at or close to the bottom of the social ladder, Paul's churches must have drawn from a relatively small group, one we might call the middle class. These were the entrepreneurs. "The 'typical' Christian, however, the one who most often signals his presence in the letters [of Paul] by one or another small clue, is a free artisan or small trader." (*Ibid.*)

Cities were a warren of small shops and work places with open spaces, here and there, used for markets. All of these had to be supplied and staffed. Much of this was done by those foreign to the city, the *metoikoi*. "For a very long time groups of foreigners had gathered in each city: merchants and artisans...in search of better markets or better access to transportation...." (Meeks, *op. cit.* p. 13) Paul himself was an example of the itinerant artisan. A tentmaker, he prided himself on always earning his own keep. "You remember our labor and toil, brothers and sisters; we worked night and day, so that we might not burden any of you while we proclaimed to you the gospel of God." (I Thessalonians 2:9) His long-time companions and fellow tent-makers (Acts 18:3) "would fit the picture of fairly well-off artisans and tradespeople." (Meeks, *op. cit.* p. 65)

That Christians would be drawn from this group is not surprising since it is the itinerant foreigners who often brought their religious beliefs with them. "The ways in which the movement of artisans and tradespeople could facilitate movements of religious cults were manifold." (*Ibid.* p. 18) Christianity followed the trade routes that led from Palestine to the rest of the empire. As a Jewish sect it moved first among the Jews and later among the Gentile traders and artisans.

B. Upper Class Christians

But not all the urban Christians were of modest means. "Thus we find Christians in the *familia Caesaris*[1] [Philippians 4:22], whose members were so often among the few upwardly mobile people in the Roman empire. We find, too, other probable freedmen or descendants of freedmen who have advanced in wealth and position, especially in the Roman colonies of Corinth and Philippi. We find wealthy artisans and traders: high in income, low in occupational prestige. We find wealthy, independent women." (Meeks, *op. cit.* p. 73) Gaius (I Corinthians 1:14; Romans 16:23) had a house ample enough to host a local church in Corinth and there would have had to be similar hosts to the local churches of other cities. Crispus (I Corinthians 1:14; Acts 18:8) is a Jew of prominence and wealth. Phoebe, "a deacon of the church at Cenchreae...a benefactor of many and of myself as well" (Romans 16:1,2), appears to be an independent woman of some means.

What would have drawn such people to the Christian community, most of whose members were in much more modest circumstances? Meeks asks: "May we further guess that the sorts of status inconsistency we observed—independent women with moderate wealth, Jews with wealth in a pagan society, freedmen with skill and money but stigmatized by origin, and so on—brought with them not only anxiety but also loneliness, in a society in which social position was important and usually rigid? Would, then, the intimacy of the Christian groups become a welcome refuge...?" (*Op. cit.* p. 191) Such well-to-do church members were not numerous but their role was crucial. "Some of the wealthy provided housing, meeting places, and other services for individual Christians and for whole groups. In effect, they filled the role of patrons." (*Ibid.* p. 73)

C. Class Conflict

Yet, as Paul's letters reveal, the disparity of wealth in these urban churches created problems. Paul admonishes the Corinthians, "When you come together, it is not really to eat the Lord's supper. For when the time comes to eat, each of you goes ahead with your own supper, and one goes hungry and another becomes drunk. What! Do you not have homes to eat and drink in? Or do you show contempt for the church of God and humiliate those who have nothing?" (I Corinthians 11:20–22) Apparently, the insensitivity of wealthier Christians led to the embarrassment of less affluent church members. The passage may reflect the custom of a host serving poorer food and wine to guests of lesser social status than to more exalted guests. Obviously, Paul felt such discrimination had no place in a Christian gathering.

In I Corinthians (chapters 8,10) Paul has an extended discussion about eating meat offered to idols. Meat was expensive and rare in the diet of all but the well-to-do. Since a common source of meat was the pagan sacrifice, a wealthy Christian could scandalize the poorer members of the community by being seen eating meat; hence Paul's concern: "But when you thus sin against members of your family, and wound their conscience when it is weak, you sin against Christ. Therefore, if food is a cause of their falling, I will never eat meat, so that I may not cause one of them to fall." (I Corinthians 8:12–13) It is easy to imagine disparity of wealth and social position placing considerable strain on life in these early Christian communities.

D. Women in the Church

Women certainly played a significant role in the Pauline communities. Many were wives in Christian families. However, a considerable number of women in the urban population were either unmarried or widowed and among them were those who had some degree of wealth and independence. Lefkowitz and Fant in their *Women's Life in Greece and Rome* list a wide range of women's occupations (pp. 161–171). They include physicians, nurses, artists, teachers, stenographers, seamstresses, to name but a few. Some of these independent women became Christians and made a significant contribution to the early churches.

Such a role for women is revealed when Paul writes to the Philippians, "I urge Euodia and I urge Syntyche to be of the same mind in the Lord. Yes, and I ask you also, my loyal companion, help these women, for they have struggled beside me in the work of the gospel." (4:2–3) Then there are women Paul mentions in writing to the Romans: Phoebe (16:1), his old friend Prisca (16:3) and his relative Junia (1:7). Also saluted are Tryphaena and Tryphosa, the mother of Rufus, Julia and the sister of Nereus. (16:12,13,15)

What is reflected in the apostle's letter to Rome was true of the role of women in other Christian communities. In fact, women seem to have played an important part in many of the mystery religions contemporary with Christianity. One factor that may have contributed to the number of women among the Christians was that the very popular sect of Mithra did not admit female members.

It is also possible that the presence of these independent women was not an unmixed blessing in the early churches. Paul writes to Corinth, "Women should be silent in the churches. For they are not permitted to speak, but should be subordinate, as the law also says." (I Corinthians 14:34) One wonders what prompted such a reactionary remark from Paul. Would these independent women have upset the more traditional Christians in the Corinthian church? Paul, always sensitive to the unity among Christians, might have sought to restrain the women in the name of peace.

The Pauline churches present a complex, diverse and even unruly picture of Christian life. Having to deal with such communities accounts for Paul's frequent appeals for unity among his readers: "We, who are many, are one body in Christ, and individually we are members one of another.... Live in harmony with one another; do not be haughty, but associate with the lowly; do not claim to be wiser than you are." (Romans 12:5,16) Chief symbols of this unity were baptism, "For in the one Spirit we were all baptized into one body—Jews or Greeks, slaves or free—" (I Corinthians 12:13) and the Lord's supper, "Because there is one bread, we who are many are one body, for we all partake of the one bread." (10:17)

III. THE MARCAN CHURCHES

A. A Gentile Community

As we have seen, the original Christians were Jewish converts. Their numbers and influence varied from community to community but generally decreased as time passed. Mark's Gospel clearly addresses Christians who have little knowledge of Judaism. How else explain the necessity of informing his readers of an obvious aspect of Jewish life? "For the Pharisees, and all the Jews, do not eat unless they thoroughly wash their hands, thus observing the tradition of the elders; and they do not eat anything from the market unless they wash it; and there are also many other traditions that they observe, the washing of cups, pots, and bronze kettles." (7:3-4) These are hardly things that would have to be explained to a Jewish reader or to anyone closely associated with Jews.

Other evidence of a Gentile community would be Mark's mention of a woman initiating divorce proceedings. (10:12) Though such was possible among the Gentiles, it was not so among the Jews and it may not have been so among the more conservative Christian communities as well. The Gospel of Matthew is addressed to a church with strong ties to Judaism. In the passage which parallels Mark on the matter of divorce (Matthew 19:7-9) there is no mention of a woman divorcing her husband.

In Mark, Aramaic expressions, such as *Boanerges* (3:17), *Talitha cum* (5:41), *Corban* (7:11), *Bartimaeus* (10:46) and *Eloi, Eloi, lema sabachthani* (15:34) are interpreted for the reader. Many Jews spoke Aramaic at the time; most probably understood it. Were there a large number of Jews in Mark's community these translations would not likely have been necessary.

At an early point in Jesus' public life, Mark has the following passage: "Jesus departed with his disciples to the sea, and a great multitude from Galilee followed him; hearing all that he was doing, they came to him in great numbers from Judea, Jerusalem, Idumea, beyond the Jordan, and the region around Tyre and Sidon." (3:7–8) The picture Mark presents is not only one of Jews flocking to Jesus but also of people coming to him from the Gentile areas to the east and to the north of Palestine, a foreshadowing of those Gentiles who will later come to believe in Jesus.

B. *Individual Gentiles*

1. THE GERASENE DEMONIAC

In the first Gospel, as in the ones that follow, the focus of Jesus' own mission was the people of Israel. In Matthew's Gospel this is made clear when Jesus says, "I was sent only to the lost sheep of the house of Israel." (15:24) However, in Mark there are four instances when Jesus does deal with Gentiles. Given the Gospel's Gentile readership these meetings are most important. The first occurs when Jesus journeys to the country of the Gerasenes.

The exact location of this territory is disputed but the presence of swine and their herders (5:11,14) clearly indicates that Jesus was among Gentiles when he met "a man out of the tombs with an unclean spirit." (5:2) The unfortunate man could not be restrained. "Night and day among the tombs and on the mountains he was always howling and bruising himself with stones." (5:5) Jesus expels the unclean spirit, but he does accede to its request to be cast into the nearby herd of swine. These destroy themselves by plunging into the lake. (5:13)

The incident closes with the following: "As [Jesus] was getting into the boat, the man who had been possessed by demons begged him that he might be with him. But Jesus refused, and said to him, 'Go home to your friends, and tell them how much the Lord has done for you, and what mercy he has shown you.' And he went away and began to proclaim in the Decapolis how much Jesus had done for him; and everyone was amazed." (5:18–20) Jesus usually demanded silence of those he cured but here we have a Gentile literally commissioned to go to a

Gentile region and spread the word, apparently successfully, a reaffirmation of the Gentile mission in early Christianity.

2. THE SYROPHOENICIAN WOMAN

Another Gentile is the Syrophoenician woman whom he encounters in Tyre. "She begged [Jesus] to cast the demon out of her daughter. He said to her, 'Let the children be fed first, for it is not fair to take the children's food and throw it to the dogs.' But she answered him, 'Sir, even the dogs under the table eat the children's crumbs.' Then he said to her, 'For saying that, you may go—the demon has left your daughter.'" (7:26–29) Jesus almost harshly states the priority of his mission to the Jews, but the woman's clever and resourceful reply moves Jesus to grant her request. Similarly, it is the faith of the Gentile Christians which brings them Jesus' favor.

3. THE DEAF MUTE

Immediately after the above Jesus returns to the Gentile region of the Decapolis. "They brought to him a deaf man who had an impediment in his speech; and they begged him to lay his hand on him." (7:32) Jesus cures the man and "ordered them to tell no one; but the more he ordered them, the more zealously they proclaimed it. They were astounded beyond measure, saying, 'He has done everything well; he even makes the deaf to hear and the mute to speak.'" (7:36–37) Seeing the cure, the Gentiles express their belief in Jesus. Again, the Gentile mission is affirmed.

4. THE CENTURION

The final and, perhaps, the most significant Gentile in Mark is the centurion who was at the foot of the cross when Jesus died. "Now when the centurion, who stood facing him, saw that in this way he breathed his last, he said, 'Truly this man was God's Son!'" (15:39) Though on two occasions (1:11; 9:7) a voice from heaven identifies Jesus as the beloved Son, the only human being echoing that statement is the centurion. He makes what is for Mark an essential act of faith without having seen one of Jesus' remarkable cures. Indeed, the centurion witnesses what must have been the most degrading moment of Jesus' career.

It would be difficult to find a more representative Roman figure. In that idealized past when all the Roman male citizenry were seen as soldiers, the basic unit was the "100" led by its centurion. As was the centurion, Mark's Christians were Gentiles. Like him also, they had not seen Jesus' wondrous deeds nor heard his words. Yet, Mark's Christians shared the centurion's act of faith: "Truly this man was God's Son!" The ideal Roman is an ideal Christian.

C. A Gentile Multitude

In Mark there are two accounts of Jesus being able to feed a vast crowd of people with a small amount of food (6:35–43; 8:2–9). On the first occasion we have five thousand men (the women and children are uncounted) satisfied by five loaves of bread and two fish. Later, four thousand people are fed with seven loaves and a few fish. In each account Jesus breaks the bread and gives it to the disciples to distribute, an expression generally regarded as reminiscent of the Lord's supper. (I Corinthians 11:24–25; Mark 14:22) Granting this, these remarkable events are a way for Mark to emphasize the spiritual benefits of the central Christian ritual.

Some scholars regard these accounts as a repeated telling of the same incident. Nevertheless, there are significant variations. For one, the locations are different. The first takes place in Galilee. The traditional site lies not far from the shore of the lake. The second, on the other hand, follows the cure of the deaf mute in the region of Decapolis and takes place in that same Gentile area. Does Mark have in mind two eucharists, one that of the more conservative Christians, still influenced by the Jewish heritage, and the other that of his Gentile Christians?

There is additional evidence that this is the case. After the first feeding of the multitude we are told that "they took up twelve baskets full of broken pieces and of the fish." (6:43) After the second, "they took up the broken pieces left over, seven baskets full." (8:8) "Twelve" is generally regarded as a "Jewish number," reflecting the twelve sons of Jacob and the twelve tribes named after them. On the other hand, "seven" might be seen as particularly Gentile, since their cosmos was ruled by the seven planets named after the seven major deities of the traditional religion. Mark's community would not have needed to be reminded of this since the days of the week were also dedicated to these divinities.

By having these two versions of the multiplication of the loaves and fishes, Mark may be reassuring his Gentile community that their Lord's supper is on a par with the rituals of other, more conservative, Christian churches. In the following chapter, we will discuss the possibility that such a rival community did exist in Rome.

IV. WHO ARE THE DISCIPLES IN MARK?

A. *Those Taught by Jesus*

Mark presents Jesus as a teacher who has gathered about himself a group of followers referred to usually as disciples. "Disciple" is the usual translation of the Greek *matheteno*, meaning one who follows the teaching of another. In this Jesus of Nazareth would have appeared to his contemporaries as a "rabbi," the Aramaic for "master." And so he is called by Peter (9:5; 11:21) and by Judas (14:45). However, for the author of the first Gospel, the more immediate model for Jesus and his disciples would have been the philosopher surrounded by his students, a sight common in any *forum*.

Mark certainly preserves traditions about these first disciples of Jesus. However, as Daniel J. Harrington, S.J. notes: "Mark's presentation of the earliest disciples was based on the parallelism between them and the members of his community." (*NJBC*, p. 597b #4) Such being the case, Mark is at times critical of his own community and the focus appears to be the inability of some to understand Jesus' message. (4:13; 6:52; 7:18; 8:17; 9:32)

One example is their failure to comprehend the meaning of the feedings of the multitudes mentioned above. After the first occasion, we are told, the disciples "did not understand about the loaves, but their hearts were hardened." (6:52) After the second feeding, Jesus bitterly complains: "'Do you still not perceive or understand? Are your hearts hardened? Do you have eyes, and fail to see? Do you have ears, and fail to hear? And do you not remember? When I broke the five loaves for the five thousand, how many baskets full of broken pieces did you collect?' They said to him, 'Twelve.' 'And the seven for the four thousand, how many baskets full of broken pieces did you collect?' And they said to him, 'Seven.' Then he said to them, 'Do you not yet understand?'"

(8:17–21) It would seem that Mark felt his community had difficulty grasping his reassurance about the value of their Lord's supper.

Perhaps more crucial was Mark's view that his readers failed to understand something very central to Jesus' message. "[Jesus] was teaching his disciples, saying to them, 'The Son of Man is to be betrayed into human hands, and they will kill him, and three days after being killed, he will rise again.' But they did not understand what he was saying and were afraid to ask him." (9:31–32) As we will see, Peter himself and the principal apostles, James and John, will fail similarly. Were there Christians who doubted the reality of Jesus' death and resurrection?

Certainly there were early Christians for whom Jesus' death was a challenge to their faith in him. Such would have been particularly true for those who had witnessed the cruel and degrading reality of crucifixions. We have evidence that Christians were mocked on this very point. A second century Roman *graffitus* has been unearthed crudely depicting a crucified figure with a donkey's head. The caption is "Alexamenos worships his god." The temptation would have been to gloss over the actuality of the event. Again we see the importance of the centurion at the foot of the cross. A witness to the crucifixion, he nevertheless expresses a fundamental faith in Jesus.

B. The "Strong" and the "Weak"

As we saw, Paul's letters at times reflect a tension between Christians of differing social status. A similar tension in Mark's own community may be seen when, at one point, Jesus "took a little child and put it among them; and taking it in his arms, he said to them, 'Whoever welcomes one such child in my name welcomes me, and whoever welcomes me welcomes not me but the one who sent me.'" (9:37) Might not the child represent the more humble members of the Christian community, those scorned by the more sophisticated?

Something similar may lie behind another scene in the Gospel: "People were bringing little children to him in order that he might touch them; and the disciples spoke sternly to them. But when Jesus saw this, he was indignant and said to them, 'Let the little children come to me; do not stop them; for it is to such as these that the kingdom of God belongs.'" (10:13–14) Again, we have Mark admonishing the more elite Christians not to denigrate the less cosmopolitan.

The possibility that such elite might scandalize the less so by their actions may also be behind Jesus' very harsh warning, "If any of you put a stumbling block before one of these little ones who believe in me, it would be better for you if a great millstone were hung around your neck and you were thrown into the sea." (9:42) Mark's community, drawing from diverse social *strata*, may have had to face a problem seen earlier in the Pauline churches.

Paul in writing to Rome cautions, "We who are strong ought to put up with the failings of the weak, and not to please ourselves." (15:1) Paul's concern was that those who felt free to eat meat sacrificed to idols would scandalize, even scorn, those who didn't. "Those who eat must not despise those who abstain, and those who abstain must not pass judgment on those who eat; for God has welcomed them." (14:3) The matter is serious. "If your brother or sister is being injured by what you eat, you are no longer walking in love. Do not let what you eat cause the ruin of one for whom Christ died." (14:15) Mark may be showing the same concern over a similar problem.

C. The Wealthy

As we noted earlier, some members of Mark's community must have had sufficient means to support the church's activities. However, these were few in number since a wealthy person would have been handicapped by becoming a Christian. Such a choice would bar the person from most of the city's social and political life. The barrier of wealth may be behind Mark's account of Jesus' encounter with the wealthy man.

"Good Teacher, what must I do to inherit eternal life?" (10:17) asks the man. When he is told by Jesus to keep the commandments, he replies, "Teacher, I have kept all these since my youth." (10:20) Jesus is impressed by such a display of virtue: "Jesus, looking at him, loved him and said, 'You lack one thing; go, sell what you own, and give the money to the poor, and you will have treasure in heaven; then come, follow me.' When [the rich man] heard this, he was shocked and went away grieving, for he had many possessions." (10:21–22) It is likely that there were virtuous Romans whose "many possessions" kept them from joining the Christian community.

Jesus continues in the same vein: "'How hard it will be for those who have wealth to enter the kingdom of God!' And the disciples were perplexed at these words. But Jesus said to them again, 'Children, how hard it is to enter the kingdom of God! It is easier for a camel to go through the eye of a needle than for someone who is rich to enter the kingdom of God." (10:23–25) To Mark's readers the barrier of wealth and position must have appeared virtually insurmountable to becoming a follower of Jesus.

Yet, humble as their circumstances may have been, Mark's readers would have been infinitely better off than most of Rome's populace caught up, as they were, in crushing poverty. From this perspective, Mark's Christians might well have raised a question similar to Peter's: "Then who can be saved?" (10:26) Jesus' reply reminds the reader of a fundamental truth: "For mortals it is impossible, but not for God; for God all things are possible." (10:26–27) Ultimately, it is not a matter of wealth or the lack of it; it is God who saves.

Some in Mark's community did, no doubt, make sacrifices to become followers of Jesus. Some suffered financial losses. Others were ostracized by family and friends. All had to abandon any role in the public life of the city. Again they might have echoed Peter: "Look, we have left everything and followed you." (10:28) In Jesus' reply, Mark reminds his readers of what is gained by following Jesus: "Truly I tell you, there is no one who has left house or brothers or sisters or mother or father or children or fields, for my sake and for the sake of the good news, who will not receive a hundredfold now in this age— houses, brothers and sisters, mothers and children, and fields with per- secutions—and in the age to come eternal life." (10:29–30)

D. The Women in Mark

1. A FAVORABLE PRESENTATION

Women are presented by Mark in a particularly favorable light. We have the woman with a hemorrhage whose faith elicits a cure from Jesus. (5:25–33) We have already mentioned the woman "of Syrophoenician origin," whose clever reply moves Jesus to heal her daughter. (7:25–29) An unknown woman anoints Jesus at the banquet in Bethany and he says of her: "She has anointed my body beforehand for its burial. Truly I tell you, wherever the good news is proclaimed in the whole world, what she has done will be told in remembrance of her." (14:8–9) No other figure in the Gospel receives such an accolade. Perhaps most significant is the presence of women at the scene of Jesus' execution where his male followers are conspicuously absent: "There were also women looking on from a distance; among them were Mary Magdalene, and Mary the mother of James the younger and of Joses, and Salome. These used to follow him and provided for him when he was in Galilee; and there were many other women who had come up with him to Jerusalem." (15:40–41) Mark's picture of Jesus in the midst of these women who supported him during his public life is in contrast to our usual vision of Jesus as surrounded only by men.

These women are more than simply spectators; they have a crucial role to play. Since they knew where Jesus had been buried (15:47) they are the link between the crucifixion and the resurrection. On the day following the sabbath two of their number, Mary Magdalene and Mary the mother of Joses, return to anoint Jesus' body. (16:1) When the tomb is found empty, they are told: "Do not be alarmed; you are looking for Jesus of Nazareth, who was crucified. He has been raised; he is not here." (16:6) The empty tomb was for the early church conclusive evidence of the resurrection. In Mark, the women are the sole witnesses to this fact. Their role is particularly important in the first Gospel as Mark does not record an appearance of the risen Christ.[2]

2. AUTHOR OF THE FIRST GOSPEL

The positive picture of Jesus' female followers, especially when compared to Mark's unfavorable depiction of Jesus' closest male companions, raises an interesting possibility. Could the Gospel's author be a woman? Speaking of women authors in the Roman period, Mary R. Lefkowitz and Maureen B. Fant note: "It is then both logical and poignant that we should have so little of what women wrote. Surviving fragments and references in the work of male authors are tantalizing indications that the intellectual efforts of women were, at least occasionally, committed to writing." (*Op. cit.* p. 3) The authors cite the unfortunate mother of Nero (he had her killed), Aggripina the Younger, "who wrote the story of her life and her family in sufficient detail to have been of use to the historian Tacitus, who cites the work." (*Op. cit.* p. 159) Still the evidence is far too slim to come to any definitive conclusion as to Mark having been written by a woman.

E. Those Challenged To Have Faith

Mark's community certainly experienced stormy times. Like the rest of Rome's population they must have suffered in the civil strife that so often marred the life of the empire's capital. We have already noted the traumatic effect on these Christians of the Jewish war and its disastrous outcome. Many were foreigners and very few had the status or the protection of Roman citizenship. Their religious exclusivity made their circumstances just that much more precarious. That, at times, their trust in Jesus was shaken would not be surprising. Mark's Gospel has a scene that may have been his way of reassuring his readers.

An early symbol for the church was a boat with Jesus and his disciples on board.

> And leaving the crowd behind, [the disciples] took [Jesus] with them in the boat, just as he was. Other boats were with him. A great windstorm arose, and the waves beat into the boat, so that the boat was already being swamped. But he was in the stern, asleep on the cushion; and they woke him up and said to him, "Teacher, do you not care that we are perishing?" He woke up and rebuked the wind, and said to the sea, "Peace! Be still!" Then the wind ceased, and there was a dead calm. He said to them, "Why are you afraid? Have you still no faith?" And they were filled with great awe and said to one another, "Who then is this, that even the wind and the sea obey him?" (4:36–41)

Mark thus encourages his storm-tossed readers to trust in Jesus. As we will see, Mark believes that there are even darker days ahead. What is coming will demand of his readers an even greater trust in the salvific power of Jesus. Indeed, we might say that the underlying motive for the writing of the first Gospel was to inspire in Mark's Christians a trust that will sustain them as history itself comes to an end.

STUDY QUESTIONS

1. To what social groups might many of Paul's Christians have belonged?
2. Were there Christians from the wealthier classes?
3. What crucial role would these Christians have played?
4. Is there evidence of friction between the poorer and wealthier Christians?
5. What were the roles women played in the early Christian communities?
6. What was one outstanding characteristic of the Marcan community?
7. What do the incidents of the Gerasene Demoniac, the Syrophoenician Woman and the Deaf Mute have in common and why is this important?
8. Which witness to Jesus' execution is the model for the faithful Christian?
9. What is significant about the second miracle of the loaves and fishes?
10. In what way might Mark's negative treatment of the disciples reflect a failure of Mark's own community?
11. In what passage of his Gospel does Mark indicate a problem of scandal in his community?
12. Did Mark feel that wealth created a special problem for the Christian and where is this indicated?
13. How are women depicted in the first Gospel?
14. What Gospel image might reflect life in Mark's community?

Chapter Five

LEADERSHIP AND RIVALRY

I. COMMUNITY LEADERSHIP

A. *The Hosts*

As Meeks notes: "No group can persist for any appreciable time without developing some patterns of leadership, some differentiation of roles among its members, some means of managing conflict, some ways of articulating shared values and norms, and some sanctions to assure acceptable levels of conformity to those norms." (*Op. cit.* p. 111) We have little information on the development of leadership roles in the earliest Christian communities. Meeks suggests: "The head of the household, by normal expectations of the society, would exercise some authority over the group and would have some legal responsibility for it." (*Ibid.* p. 76) Those hosting either a house church or a local church would not have been limited to men. Branick concludes that "we can place Nympha with Prisca and Lydia, as heads of house churches in the Pauline world of Christianity." (*Op. cit.* p. 76)

Mark's communities would have also needed a host for their local church, or a hostess for that matter. It is also quite possible that it was that same person who financed the reproduction and even distribution of the first Gospel. Given the expense involved in copying and then circulating a manuscript a wealthy person would be needed to support such an enterprise. Whoever that unknown person was, Christianity owes her or him a great debt of gratitude.

B. *The Apostles*

1. IN THE PAULINE CHURCHES

"In effect two sources of administrative authority existed in the Pauline churches. On the one hand, the hosts and patrons literally had the 'power of the keys.' On the other hand, apostles, prophets, and teachers could speak as interpreters of the divine will. The host-patrons were linked to the house church. The apostles, prophets, and teachers represented the larger church." (Branick, *ibid.* p. 93). We have a prime example of one such apostle: "Paul an apostle—sent neither by human commission nor from human authorities, but through Jesus Christ and God the Father." (Galatians 1:1) It is a position he vigorously defends in writing to the Corinthians: "Am I not an apostle? Have I not seen Jesus our Lord? Are you not my work in the Lord? If I am not an apostle to others, at least I am to you; for you are the seal of my apostleship in the Lord." (I Corinthians 9:1–2)

Paul is not the only apostle; he is not the only one "sent," the meaning of the Greek word *apostolos*. Peter has a parallel role: "For he who worked through Peter making him an apostle to the circumcised also worked through me in sending me to the Gentiles." (Galatians 2:8) The resurrected Christ appears to "the twelve" as well as to all the apostles (I Corinthians 15:5,7) before his appearance to Paul, "as to one untimely born." (15:8)

There emerges as well a similarly designated role in the Christian community. "God has appointed in the church first apostles, second prophets, third teachers...."(12:28) There is even evidence that a woman could be an apostle. One "Junia" is said by Paul to be "prominent among the apostles." (Romans 16:7) As Meeks observes: "The earlier apostles, in Paul's terms, were in fact a large and, as far as we can see, not well–defined group." (*Op. cit.* p. 132)

Unfortunately, the roles of prophets and teachers at this early stage are even less well-defined. They could have been locally recognized figures or, like the apostles, have moved from city to city. Whatever is the case, they are evidence that these first churches were not isolated one from another. Apostles and others constantly circulated the basic Christian message among the churches of the empire.

2. IN MARK'S COMMUNITY

a. A Role Respected

The only clues to the role apostles may have played in Mark's church are found in the Gospel's treatment of the apostles. They are shown as figures of considerable prestige. Four of them are directly recruited by Jesus; these are Simon [Peter], Andrew and the Zebedees, James and John (1:16–20). Then the twelve are formally selected: "And he appointed twelve, whom he also named apostles, to be with him, and to be sent out to proclaim the message." (3:14). They are listed as: "Simon (to whom he gave the name Peter); James son of Zebedee and John the brother of James (to whom he gave the name Boanerges, that is, Sons of Thunder); and Andrew, and Philip, and Bartholomew, and Matthew, and Thomas, and James son of Alphaeus, and Thaddaeus, and Simon the Cananaean, and Judas Iscariot, who betrayed him." (3:16–19).

Mark also gives a description of the manner in which the twelve are to carry out their ministry:

> [Jesus] called the twelve and began to send them out two by two, and gave them authority over the unclean spirits. He ordered them to take nothing for their journey except a staff; no bread, no bag, no money in their belts; but to wear sandals and not to put on two tunics. He said to them, "Wherever you enter a house, stay there until you leave the place. If any place will not welcome you and they refuse to hear you, as you leave, shake off the dust that is on your feet as a testimony against them." So they went out and proclaimed that all should repent. They cast out many demons, and anointed with oil many who were sick and cured them. (6:7–13)

Mark's vision of the apostolic mission is most likely idealized. His description of the apostles as dependent on the generosity of those who welcome them may have reminded Mark's readers of another group. Josephus says of the Essenes:[1] "When [Essenes] arrive from elsewhere, all local resources are put at their disposal as if they were their own, and men they have never seen before entertain them like old friends. And so when they travel they carry no baggage at all....In every town one of the order is appointed specially to look after strangers and issue clothing and provisions." (*Op. cit.* pp. 133–134). Itinerant Christian apostles visiting Mark's community would have been shown a similar hospitality.

Mark does not question the authority of the apostles. When Jesus says, "Whoever welcomes one such child in my name welcomes me, and whoever welcomes me welcomes not me but the one who sent me" (9:37), the context indicates that the "child" is an apostle. Yet, in spite of the obvious prestige Mark accords the apostles, he also presents a disparaging picture of them.

b. A Role Criticized

First there is Simon, the leader of the twelve, and given the name "Peter"[2] by Jesus. (3:16) Peter speaks for the apostolic group when he correctly identifies Jesus as the Messiah (8:29). But then Jesus tells of his own approaching fate: "... the Son of Man must undergo great suffering, and be rejected by the elders, the chief priests, and the scribes,[3] and be killed, and after three days rise again." (8:31) When Jesus says this quite openly, "Peter took him aside and began to rebuke him." (8:32) Aware that the disciples have witnessed the rebuke, Jesus delivers a crushing admonition, "Get behind me, Satan! For you are setting your mind not on divine things but on human things." (8:33)

The apostles James and John also rank high among the twelve. They, along with Peter, are witnesses to Jesus' transfiguration. (9:2) Later, Jesus describes in greater detail what is to happen: "See, we are going up to Jerusalem, and the Son of Man will be handed over to the chief priests and the scribes, and they will condemn him to death; then they will hand him over to the Gentiles; they will mock him, and spit upon him, and flog him, and kill him; and after three days he will rise again." (10:33–34) Yet at this very point: "James and John, the sons of Zebedee, came forward to him and said to him, 'Teacher, we want you to do for us whatever we ask of you.'" (10:35) Their request displays their seeming indifference to what Jesus has just said: "Grant us to sit, one at your right hand and one at your left, in your glory." (10:37) The closest advisors to a ruler were those who "had his ear," i.e. those sitting beside him. James and John aspired to these positions of influence.

Not surprisingly, their attempted power grab upset the rest of Jesus' followers. (10:41) When these same followers are earlier shown arguing about who among them is the greatest, Jesus sat down, called the twelve, and said to them, "Whoever wants to be first must be last of all and servant of all." (9:35) All of the apostles are put in their place by Jesus.

As we will see in the final period of Jesus' life Peter and James and John cannot remain awake to pray with him (14:37). Judas betrays him, all desert him and even Peter denies knowing Jesus. Why this mixture of prestige and censure in Mark's portrayal of Jesus' closest companions? It may be part of the tradition he received since it is difficult to imagine Mark simply creating so devastating a picture of Jesus' original followers. Yet, such a depiction of the apostles may have served Mark's purposes.

II. A RIVAL LOCAL CHURCH

A. *One More Apostolic*

In Paul's letter to the Christians of Corinth he indicates there were divisions in the community there: "For it has been reported to me by Chloe's people that there are quarrels among you, my brothers and sisters. What I mean is that each of you says, 'I belong to Paul,' or 'I belong to Apollos,' or 'I belong to Cephas,' or 'I belong to Christ.'" (I Corinthians 1:11–12) The apostle may be suggesting rivalries between house churches, perhaps stemming from their being evangelized by different missionaries. House churches sharing the same founder may have also met together as a local church. A similar situation could well have existed in Rome.

We saw that Paul's letter to the Roman Christians reflected a community of both Jews and non-Jews, a combination missing in Mark's obviously Gentile church. Was there a schism between the more and the less Jewish house churches? If so, Mark could have faced a rival local church, perhaps one asserting greater prestige. It might have been a community claiming Peter as a founder as did a group in Corinth. Mark does not deny apostolic authority, but he certainly dims the renown of Jesus' first companions.

Raymond Brown believes that the New Testament documents, I Peter and Hebrews, were written to Roman Christians, dating them "between the late 60s and early 90s, with the suspicion that both may belong to the 80s." (*Antioch and Rome*, p. 128) The community or communities these works reflect may well have been contemporaries of Mark. Brown speaks of them as "befitting a church with a strong attachment to the Jewish heritage." (*Ibid.* p. 158) Such a local church would have clearly been in opposition to the Christian community we see reflected in Mark.

Earlier, we noted the two occasions on which Jesus multiplied the loaves and fishes, scenes reminiscent of the Lord's supper. The leftovers of one filled twelve baskets, the other, seven. A possibility is that the former represented a Christian community with, as Brown puts it, "a strong attachment to the Jewish heritage," hence the number twelve. The latter would have been the community of Mark, seven being, as we said, a pagan or Gentile number.

B. One More Conservative

The Roman community to which Paul wrote appears also to have been divided on dietary matters and the apostle urges tolerance:

> Some believe in eating anything, while the weak eat only vegetables. Those who eat must not despise those who abstain, and those who abstain must not pass judgment on those who eat; for God has welcomed them.... I know and am persuaded in the Lord Jesus that nothing is unclean in itself; but it is unclean for anyone who thinks it unclean. If your brother or sister is being injured by what you eat, you are no longer walking in love. Do not let what you eat cause the ruin of one for whom Christ died. (14:2–3,14–15)

We find no such nuanced expression in Mark: "'Then do you also fail to understand? Do you not see that whatever goes into a person from outside cannot defile, since it enters, not the heart but the stomach, and goes out into the sewer?' (Thus [Jesus] declared all foods clean.)" (7:18–19) It is as simple as that. Mark's community could have been similarly liberal on other matters, putting them at variance with their more conservative rival.

If such was the situation then it is possible that the evangelist's treatment of the Pharisees actually reflects his view of these more conservative Christians. The Pharisees—the title means "separate ones"—appeared about 150 years before Christ. Lay, rather than priestly, they sought to make the Jewish religion something that could be part of daily life. In addition to the Torah, they recognized tradition as also normative. Josephus describes them as "a Jewish sect that appeared more pious than the rest and stricter in interpretation of the Law." (*Op. cit.* p. 42) Mark may well be preserving the tradition of an understandable conflict between the Pharisees and Jesus.

Yet, would Mark's Gentile community be concerned about a conservative Jewish sect? Is it not possible that the Gospel reflects the evangelist's opposition to a rival, more conservative, Christian community? Such a community might have leveled the same charge at Mark's church as the Pharisees leveled at Jesus: "Why do your disciples not live according to the tradition of the elders?" (7:5)

In accepting Gentiles without requiring them to observe any of the Jewish law, Mark's community must have seemed overly lax to their rival Christians. In the Gospel Jesus defends the more liberal policy: "Those who are well have no need of a physician, but those who are sick; I have come to call not the righteous but sinners." (2:17) The two Christian groups may have also differed on the sabbath observance. Mark's Jesus sets the proper priority: "The sabbath was made for humankind, and not humankind for the sabbath." (2:27)

In one respect, Mark's community may have been more restrictive. Reflecting Jewish tradition, the rival community may have permitted a husband to divorce his wife, though still not allowing the woman the same privilege. The first Gospel rules out divorce entirely: "Whoever divorces his wife and marries another commits adultery against her; and if she divorces her husband and marries another, she commits adultery." (10:11–12)

If our view is correct, the rival Christian community would have tried to integrate more of the Jewish traditions into their understanding of Jesus' message. In a saying of Jesus, Mark makes his position clear: "No one puts new wine into old wineskins; otherwise, the wine will burst the skins, and the wine is lost, and so are the skins; but one puts new wine into fresh wineskins." (2:22) The first Gospel represents a radical break with Judaism.

C. A Conservative Reaction

What would have been the reaction to Mark's Gospel in that more conservative Christian community? Though we are getting ahead of our story, we may have a partial answer to the question in the Gospel of Matthew. It was written some twenty or so years later than Mark and is thought to have originated in Antioch, the capital of the province of Syria. John P. Meier characterizes the unknown author as follows: "Being a true 'liberal conservative,' [Matthew] does not throw away the various strands of the old Jewish–Christian tradition." (*Antioch and Rome*, p. 59) Mark's rivals might have been an earlier version of the Christian community reflected in Matthew.

We can see in Matthew a response to Mark's rather cavalier treatment of Jewish traditions. Here Jesus says: "Do not think that I have come to abolish the law or the prophets; I have come not to abolish but to fulfill. For truly I tell you, until heaven and earth pass away, not one letter, not one stroke of a letter, will pass from the law until all is accomplished." (5:17–18) Matthew reassures those Christians in his community who still valued their Jewish heritage.

Mark simply says, "No one puts new wine into old wineskins; otherwise, the wine will burst the skins, and the wine is lost, and so are the skins; but one puts new wine into fresh wineskins." (2:22) Matthew adds a qualification: "Neither is new wine put into old wineskins; otherwise, the skins burst, and the wine is spilled, and the skins are destroyed; but new wine is put into fresh wineskins, and so *both are preserved*." (Matthew 9:17) Thus, the "old wineskins," the Jewish traditions, and the "new wine," the Gospel of Jesus, are both safeguarded.

A conservative reaction to Mark may also be seen in how Matthew seeks to balance his predecessor's negative portrayal of Peter (8:32–33). Matthew incorporates the earlier Gospel's passage where Peter correctly identifies Jesus as the Messiah. However, a crucial insertion is added: "Blessed are you, Simon son of Jonah! For flesh and blood has not revealed this to you, but my Father in heaven. And I tell you, you are Peter, and on this rock I will build my church, and the gates of Hades will not prevail against it. I will give you the keys of the kingdom of heaven, and whatever you bind on earth will be bound in heaven, and whatever you loose on earth will be loosed in heaven." (16:17–19) Peter may have failed to understand the role of Jesus, but Matthew reaffirms his authority.

We see a similar softening of the Marcan critique of the apostles

James and John. In Matthew the request for the seats of honor in the kingdom (Mark 10:35–37) is not made by the apostles themselves, but by their mother on their behalf (Matthew 20:20–21). Then, in the closing lines of Matthew's Gospel, the teaching authority of all the apostles is emphasized when Jesus says: "All authority in heaven and on earth has been given to me. Go therefore and make disciples of all nations, baptizing them in the name of the Father and of the Son and of the Holy Spirit, and teaching them to obey everything that I have commanded you. And remember, I am with you always, to the end of the age." (28:18–20)

III. LEADERSHIP IN TRANSITION

In the time between Mark and Matthew a development in community leadership roles must have taken place. When Mark was writing his Gospel, the hosts of the house or local churches, men or women, would have exercised leadership. Then, in the intervening fifteen or twenty years that separate the two evangelists a new leadership began to emerge, a leadership that drew its claim to authority from Peter and the apostles.

A similar change is also seen in Luke. His Gospel omits the passage found in Mark where Jesus admonishes Peter for failing to understand the first of the passion predictions. (8:33) Following the second such prediction, Mark states simply that the disciples did not understand what Jesus was saying. (9:23) However, Luke expands Mark with "its meaning was concealed from them, so that they could not perceive it." (9:45) Thus he exonerates Jesus' followers of fault.

In the obviously embarrassing scene where James and John request the places of honor in Jesus' kingdom, we saw that Matthew shifted the blame to their mother. (20:20) Luke simply omits the scene altogether. Moreover, the Acts of the Apostles, companion volume to Luke's Gospel, is dominated by apostolic figures, particularly Peter and Paul. The work certainly reinforces apostolic authority.

If Mark seems cavalier in attitude toward church leadership, there may be an explanation. A community characterized by the expectation of history's impending end will not be concerned over the niceties of leadership. On the other hand, one looking forward to a distant future must be concerned about the persons who will give it a secure and authoritative guidance. Such was the situation for Matthew's and Luke's communities. As we will see in the following chapter, it is precisely here that Mark differs from thc two evangelists who followed him.

STUDY QUESTIONS

1. Who would have exercised leadership in the early house and local churches?
2. How are the apostles depicted in Mark's Gospel?
3. In what way is the first Gospel critical of the apostles?
4. What were the characteristics of a local church that might have been a rival to Mark's?
5. In what way might the Gospel of Matthew be a reaction to that of Mark?
6. What change in church leadership roles took place between the writing of the Gospel of Mark and those of Matthew and Luke?

Chapter Six

THE PAROUSIA AND THE SON OF MAN

I. AN EMPIRE IN CRISIS

Kenneth Wellesley in his introduction to the *Histories of Tacitus* makes the following observation:

> The year 69, "that long but single year" as Tacitus had earlier called it, offers a wealth of dramatic incidents. After the solid and prosperous security of the first or Julio-Claudian dynasty, the ground opens. The vast edifice of the world empire is shaken. Pretender rises against pretender. The frontier armies move on Rome from Spain, Germany, the Balkans and the East. The frontiers themselves are breached by the barbarian. There are palace conspiracies, sudden assassinations, desperate battles, deeds of heroism and perfidy. The scene shifts continually from one end of the empire to the other, from Britain to Palestine, from Morocco to the Caucasus. Three emperors—Galba, Otho and Vitelius—meet their ends. The fourth, Vespasius, survives by fate or chance or merit, and founds his dynasty for good or ill. Here, in a clash of Roman with Roman, the civilized world seemed for the moment about to perish. (pp. 9–10)

It would have been in Rome itself that these events had their greatest impact. In such times of danger and disaster, expectations of an end of the world are usually enhanced. This was true for the Romans. Franz Cumont tells us in his *Oriental Religions in Roman Paganism* that the pagan religions of the period expected "the destruction of the universe, the death of the wicked, and the eternal happiness of the good in a reconstructed world." (pp. viii–ix) The author notes later: "The reign of evil would not last forever. According to the common opinion the universe would be destroyed by fire after times had been fulfilled. All the wicked would perish, but the just would be revived and establish the reign of universal happiness in the regenerated world." (*Ibid.* p. 210) Cumont credits the spread of this outlook to the Stoics, the astrologers and the mystery religions. (*Op. cit.* p. 287, ftn. 27)

The Christians living in the capital certainly shared with their pagan neighbors the trauma of "that long but single year." For them as well, "the civilized world seemed for the moment about to perish." Usually, the small entrepreneur suffers the most from civil unrest since he can easily lose all he has, with no possibility of recovery. Then, just as some measure of stability was restored under Vespasian, another disaster occurs and one of a profoundly religious character.

In 70 C.E., at the climax of the Jewish war, the walls of Jerusalem were breached by the Roman legions. In the course of the final battle there is an appalling calamity. Josephus gives us an account: "Then one of the [Roman] soldiers, without waiting for orders and without qualm for the terrible consequences of his action but urged on by some unseen force, snatched up a blazing piece of wood and hurled a brand through a golden aperture giving access on the north side to the chambers built around the Sanctuary [of the Temple]." (*Op. cit.* p. 357). In spite of efforts by both Jew and Roman, Jerusalem's temple, one of the wonders of the ancient world, was completely destroyed. It was a tragedy that sent reverberations throughout the whole empire.

II. THE JEWISH TRAUMA

As would be expected, the Jewish communities, spread throughout the empire, were the most profoundly affected both by the war and by its tragic climax. The very center of their religion was the temple in Jerusalem. For the Jew its sanctuary was the dwelling place of God. To offer sacrifice at the altar of the temple was the hope of every Jew. The Hebrew Bible is vivid testimony to the role of the temple in the history of Israel. The turmoil that must have followed its destruction is easy to imagine.

In the years following the calamity several Jewish sects disappeared from history. These were the Sadducees who had directed the activities of the temple, the Zealots who fought for Palestine's independence, and the Essenes, a Jewish sect we saw earlier. The ultimate surviving group of the Jews were the Pharisees. They were particularly prominent in the synagogues throughout the empire. After the destruction of the temple and as their influence increased, the Pharisees purged non-Pharisees from the ranks of Judaism. Among those excommunicated were Jewish Christians who had maintained their membership in the synagogues. The bitterness that resulted is frequently reflected in the documents of the New Testament as we see in Matthew (23:13,15,25,27) and Luke (14:39,41–44). In Mark, the Pharisees do oppose Jesus but have no role in Jesus' condemnation and execution.[1]

III. THE CHRISTIAN TRAUMA

In many ways, the Christian communities found the destruction of Jerusalem equally traumatic. It was there that Jesus spent his final days, there that he was executed and buried, and there that he had risen from the dead. Moreover, the Christians of Jerusalem formed the oldest and most prestigious Christian community, one that appears to have exercised some leadership in the earliest period of Christianity. (Acts 16:4) The Jerusalem Christians, according to tradition, had fled the city before its destruction.

Mark's Christians must have shared in the trauma of Jerusalem's conquest and the destruction of the temple. However, the disaster was brought home to them in a particularly vivid manner. They would have been among the vast throng that lined the streets of the city to witness the triumphant return of the victorious Titus as he marched through the capital city. "Not one person stayed at home out of the immense population of the city: everyone came out and, although there was only standing-room, found a place somewhere, so that there was barely enough room for the procession itself to pass." (Josephus, *op. cit.* p. 383)

It is easy to imagine the shock of Jesus' followers when they saw the treasures of Jerusalem's temple paraded before them: "Most of the spoils that were carried were heaped up indiscriminately, but more prominent were those captured in the Temple at Jerusalem—a gold table, and a lampstand similarly made of gold...from it extended slender branches…with the end of each forged into a lamp: these numbered seven…after these was carried the Jewish Law." (*Ibid.* p. 386) Actually, what the Romans saw can be viewed today. It is depicted by a bas–relief carved on the Arch of Titus that spans the Sacred Way in Rome's Forum.

Such a tragedy, following close upon the turmoil of the previous year, must have deeply shaken the Christians of Mark's community. If as noted the pagans were expecting "the destruction of the universe" (Cumont, *ibid.*), then how much more so would have the Christians? As Paula Fredriksen observes, "The Temple's recent destruction clearly marks the beginning of that period that will terminate with the Second Coming of the Son of Man…the Parousia[2] could occur at any time, certainly within the lifetime of Mark's community." (*Op. cit.* pp. 50–51)

In our opening chapter, we concluded that the first Gospel was composed after 70 C.E. and reflected a Christian reaction to the tragic events of that period. The expectation of the impending parousia was such a reaction. To make that anticipation understandable, Mark wove together traditions about Jesus and about the religious heritage the author of the Gospel had received from Judaism.

IV. FROM APOCALYPSE TO PAROUSIA

A. *Jewish Visions of the Future*

It was not the first time that Jerusalem had been conquered and its temple destroyed. In 587 B.C.E. the Babylonians under Nebuchadnezzar vanquished Israel and, after razing its capital city, led many of its leading citizens off to Babylon. Thus began the period known as the Exile. In the normal course of events, the people of Israel would have disappeared from history, a fate that had befallen other conquered peoples. Then, in a happenstance that must have appeared miraculous, God rescued the exiles.

Cyrus, leading the Medes and Persians, conquered the Babylonians with startling speed. Then, in 538 B.C.E., Cyrus allowed the surviving Israelites to return to Judea and begin the rebuilding of the city and its temple. Tragically, the high hopes of the Jews when they returned from Babylon were soon crushed. The realities of a destroyed capital, reduced population and grinding poverty took their toll. The restoration of the city and especially the temple proved a formidable task. The discouragement of these people is understandable.

To buoy up the Israelites' spirits, the prophets of the period painted an optimistic picture of the future. They looked beyond the immediate or near future to an end of history, to a period of glory. One such was Isaiah III.[3] "For I am about to create new heavens and a new earth; the former things shall not be remembered or come to mind." (65:17) This new creation will be a restored garden of Eden where "the wolf and the lamb shall feed together, the lion shall eat straw like the ox...."(65:25) Later, around the mid-fifth century B.C.E., the prophecy of Malachi adds another element to the vision of the future. "See, I am sending my messenger to prepare the way before me, and the Lord whom you seek will suddenly come to his temple. The messenger of the covenant in whom you delight—indeed, he is coming, says the LORD of hosts. But who can endure the day of his coming...?" (3:1–2)

As the fifth century comes to an end, the prophetic visions sound an ominous note. Joel warns, "Alas for the day! For the day of the LORD is near, and as destruction from the Almighty it comes.... Blow the trumpet in Zion; sound the alarm on my holy mountain! Let all the inhabitants of the land tremble, for the day of the LORD is coming, it is near—a day of darkness and gloom, a day of clouds and thick darkness!" (1:15; 2:1–2) Then Zechariah adds another element: "On that day the LORD will shield the inhabitants of Jerusalem so that the feeblest among them on that day shall be like David, and the house of David shall be like God, like the angel of the LORD, at their head. And on that day I will seek to destroy all the nations that come against Jerusalem.... And the LORD will become king over all the earth." (12:8–9; 14:9) The prophecy of a future kingdom of God will be particularly influential among early Christians.

When the next two and a half centuries have passed the same expectations are re-expressed. Now the Hellenistic culture has swept over the Mediterranean world following the conquests by Alexander the Great. Judea lies under the heel of the Selucid ruler, Antiochus IV

Epiphanes. Antiochus seeks to absorb the Jews into the Hellenism of his kingdom. He tries to force them to abandon their ancient religion and join in the pagan worship of his realm. The resistance of Israel to Antiochus is recorded in the story of the Maccabees.

During this period and in the years that followed, a group of writings appeared among the Jews that are called "apocalyptic" from the Greek for "revelation." John J. Collins notes: "An apocalypse is defined by both form and content: a genre of revelatory literature, mediated by an angel or heavenly being, which is concerned with a transcendent world...." (*NJBC* p. 299a) In periods of serious threat to Jewish life the apocalyptic writers, like the prophets that had preceded them, looked to the culmination of history and a final revelation of God's power. They differed from the prophets in their use of a highly symbolic language to convey their message.

Apocalyptic literature was produced among the Jews between 200 B.C.E. and 100 C.E. We know from such material as the "Dead Sea Scrolls" that many Jews at the time of Jesus had apocalyptic expectations. They faced the overwhelming power of a pagan empire that ruled the world. Their only hope was that their God would come to crush Rome and to establish his own rule, his own kingdom. Yahweh would return Israel to her former glory.

B. Paul and the Parousia

The first followers of Jesus of Nazareth, after his execution, must have faced the same discouragement as did the exiles in Babylon; like them their hope was all but gone. Then occurred the event described by the apostle Paul, "[Jesus] was raised on the third day in accordance with the scriptures, and...he appeared to Cephas, then to the twelve. Then he appeared to more than five hundred brothers and sisters at one time, most of whom are still alive, though some have died. Then he appeared to James, then to all the apostles. Last of all, as to one untimely born, he appeared also to me." (I Corinthians 15:4–8) The earliest Christians were convinced that Jesus had risen from the dead.

Moreover, they lived in the expectation that Jesus would return soon and establish God's kingdom. Paul shared this expectation as we read in the first of the letters he wrote to the Christians in Thessalonica: "For the Lord himself, with a cry of command, with the archangel's call and with the sound of God's trumpet, will descend from heaven, and the dead in Christ will rise first. Then we who are alive, who are left, will be caught up in the clouds together with them to meet the Lord in the air; and so we will be with the Lord forever." (4:16–17) This hoped-for event is usually referred to as the parousia. Like many Christians of his time, it is obvious that Paul expects to survive until the parousia, until "the coming of our Lord Jesus with all his saints." (3:13; see also 4:15; 5:23)

I Thessalonians, was written in 50 C.E. while Paul was in Corinth. Meeks notes that in this letter "the emphasis was on *waiting* for Jesus, 'who saves us from the *coming* wrath.' (1:10)" (*Op. cit.* p. 176; Meeks' emphasis) Four years later, while in Ephesus, Paul writes to the Galatians telling them that Jesus has "set us free from the present evil age." (1:4) According to Meeks: "The emphasis throughout Galatians is on the present fulfillment of eschatological hopes." (*Ibid.*) Now there is a sense in which the parousia has already occurred.

In 57 C.E., while in Ephesus, the apostle writes the first of his two letters to Corinth. He speaks again of the parousia: "... all will be made alive in Christ. But each in his own order: Christ the first fruits, then at his coming those who belong to Christ." (15:22–23) Meeks sees this as another shift in emphasis. "On the face of it, then, Paul's employment of apocalyptic categories here seems to be the reverse of that in Galatians.... Here [Paul] uses eschatological language in the future tense to restrain innovation and to counsel stability and order." (*Op. cit.* p. 179) The parousia has now become remote, something expected but lying in the distant future.

In the final authentic letter of Paul, written to the Romans in the winter of 57–58 C.E., we find apocalyptic language playing no significant role. The author's focus is on living by faith. Also, as Meeks points out, "apocalyptic language has a very small place in the pseudonymous letters to Colossians and Ephesians and therefore did not have equal, or equally enduring, significance to all members of the Pauline circle." (*Ibid.* p. 171) It would appear that as the century waned, Christian eschatological concerns lessened as well.

V. MARK AND THE PAROUSIA

A. The Signs

1. THE BIRTH PANGS

Earlier we observed that in Mark Jesus makes only a brief reference to the destruction of the temple: "As [Jesus] came out of the temple, one of his disciples said to him, 'Look, Teacher, what large stones and what large buildings!' Then Jesus asked him, 'Do you see these great buildings? Not one stone will be left here upon another; all will be thrown down.' Later, when he was sitting on the Mount of Olives opposite the temple, Peter, James, John, and Andrew asked him privately, 'Tell us, when will this be, and what will be the sign that all these things are about to be accomplished?'" (13:1–4) With the destruction of the temple fresh in his readers' minds, Mark did not have to explain in detail the disaster to which Jesus was referring. The author rather turns to other events that will culminate in the impending parousia.

"When you hear of wars and rumors of wars, do not be alarmed; this must take place, but the end is still to come. For nation will rise against nation, and kingdom against kingdom; there will be earthquakes in various places; there will be famines. This is but the beginning of the birthpangs." (13:7–8) For Mark's readers, these lines would have accurately described the empire's unrest of preceding years. Yet they were only a prelude to "that long but single year" of 69 C.E. and to the disaster of 70 C.E.

In the midst of all the turmoil, the Christians in the empire must have undergone the indignities and betrayals to which Mark refers: "As for yourselves, beware; for they will hand you over to councils; and you will be beaten in synagogues; and you will stand before governors and kings because of me.... Brother will betray brother to death, and a father his child, and children will rise against parents and have them put to death; and you will be hated by all because of my name." (13:9,12–13)

Why the delay in Jesus' return? Now some forty years have passed. Mark inserts an explanation in the above passage: "And the good news must first be proclaimed to all nations." (13:10) True, by Mark's time the number of Christians was small, but their communities were to be found in many of the empire's urban areas, including the capital itself.

Mark could have felt that the Gospel had been "proclaimed to all nations." Now the "birthpangs" had been brought to completion in the tragedy of 70 C.E.

2. THE FINAL WARNINGS

Mark depicts Jesus as foreseeing the distress of those Christians who will be in Jerusalem as the invading forces approach:

> But when you see the desolating sacrilege set up where it ought not to be (let the reader understand), then those in Judea must flee to the mountains; the one on the housetop must not go down or enter the house to take anything away; the one in the field must not turn back to get a coat. Woe to those who are pregnant and to those who are nursing infants in those days! Pray that it may not be in winter. For in those days there will be suffering, such as has not been from the beginning of the creation that God created until now, no, and never will be. And if the Lord had not cut short those days, no one would be saved; but for the sake of the elect, whom he chose, he has cut short those days. And if anyone says to you at that time, "Look! Here is the Messiah!" or "Look! There he is!"—do not believe it. False messiahs and false prophets will appear and produce signs and omens, to lead astray, if possible, the elect. (13:14–22)

The phrase "desolating sacrilege" harks back to the book of Daniel:[4] "The troops of the prince who is to come shall destroy the city and the sanctuary.... He shall make sacrifice and offering cease; and in their place shall be an abomination that desolates." (9:26,27) Mark's readers would understand that the "desolating sacrilege" was the Roman military standards carried into the temple's sanctuary. "As the partisans had fled into the city, and flames were consuming the Sanctuary itself and all its surroundings, the Romans brought their standards into the Temple area, and erecting them opposite the East Gate sacrificed to them there." (Josephus, *op. cit.* p. 363) The author is again handling delicately the Roman involvement in the Jerusalem tragedy.

The desperate situation of all the Judeans was certainly fulfilled as the Roman troops marched on the city. On the other hand, Mark's mention of "the elect" may indicate that his specific concern was for the safety of the Christians who still lived in the area. As mentioned earlier, the Jerusalem church was the earliest Christian community and of considerable prestige. Fortunately, these Christians were able to make their escape and Mark saw their being spared as an act of God. "False messiahs and false prophets" did appear among the Jews preceding and during the Jewish war, frequently with unfortunate results. (See Josephus, *op. cit.* p. 147) It would be likely that some of these exerted influence on the Christians of the period. False claimants might have come as far as Rome and have been a concern to Mark. He would have felt that his own community could fall under their aegis. Such a concern would be an additional motive for his composition of the first Gospel.

B. *The Parousia*

The turmoil in the empire, coupled with the destruction of Jerusalem and its Temple, apparently led Mark and his church to the conclusion that these were indeed signs of the approaching parousia. They would have seen the words of Jesus as being directed to them. "The time is fulfilled, and the kingdom of God has come near; repent, and believe in the good news." (1:15) Likewise, it was of them that Jesus said, "Truly I tell you, there are some standing here who will not taste death until they see that the kingdom of God has come with power." (9:1) Mark drew upon the apocalyptic language of Jewish tradition to envision what was soon to come about.

"But in those days, after that suffering, the sun will be darkened, and the moon will not give its light, and the stars will be falling from heaven, and the powers in the heavens will be shaken." (13:24–25) The prophets made frequent mention of the cosmic turmoil that will characterize the climax of history: "For the stars of the heavens and their constellations will not give their light; the sun will be dark at its rising, and the moon will not shed its light." (Isaiah 13:10) "When I blot you out, I will cover the heavens, and make their stars dark; I will cover the sun with a cloud, and the moon shall not give its light." (Ezekiel 32:7; see also Amos 8:9; Joel 2:10,31; Isaiah 34:4; Haggai 2:6,21) In the pagan cultures, the stars and planets were thought to exert a controlling influence on human life. In these cosmic signs, Mark's readers would see a testimony to their God's dominant power over the world.

"Then they will see 'the Son of Man coming in the clouds' with great power and glory. Then he will send out the angels, and gather his elect from the four winds, from the ends of the earth to the ends of heaven." (13:26–27) A final gathering of God's people is mentioned by Isaiah: "On that day the Lord will extend his hand yet a second time to recover the remnant that is left of his people, from Assyria, from Egypt, from Pathros, from Ethiopia, from Elam, from Shinar, from Hamath, and from the coastlands of the sea." (11:11; see also Isaiah 11:16 and Ezekiel 39:27) There are echoes here also of Paul's first letter to the Thessalonians: "For the Lord himself, with a cry of command, with the archangel's call and with the sound of God's trumpet, will descend from heaven, and the dead in Christ will rise first. Then we who are alive, who are left, will be caught up in the clouds together with them to meet the Lord in the air; and so we will be with the Lord forever." (4:16–17)

C. The Son of Man

1. IN THE HEBREW BIBLE

In Mark's apocalyptic vision the central figure is that of "the Son of Man." The source of this title is found in the book of Daniel: "As I watched in the night visions, I saw one like a human being[5] coming with the clouds of heaven. And he came to the Ancient One and was presented before him. To him was given dominion and glory and kingship, that all peoples, nations, and languages should serve him. His dominion is an everlasting dominion that shall not pass away, and his kingship is one that shall never be destroyed." (7:13–14) Geza Vermes states that in Daniel, "the Son of Man" is "symbolic representation of the eschatological triumph of the historical Israel." (*Jesus the Jew*, p. 170)

2. IN MARK

The title "the Son of Man" is not found in Paul's authentic letters nor in those attributed to him. Why it is employed by the author of the first Gospel is much debated. Mark may have been in possession of a tradition that Jesus referred to himself as "the Son of Man." In any event, the title links together two central themes of Mark, that of the coming parousia and, as we will see later, that of the "kingdom of

God." As noted, the book of Daniel speaks of "his [the Son of Man's] kingship" as "one that shall never be destroyed." (7:14)

In Mark, Jesus refers to himself as "the Son of Man" thirteen times. Eight times the title is used in connection with his suffering and death. "Then he began to teach them that the Son of Man must undergo great suffering, and be rejected by the elders, the chief priests, and the scribes, and be killed, and after three days rise again." (8:31; see also 9:12,31; 10:33,45; 14:21,41) Jesus also speaks of the Son of Man having the power to forgive sins (2:10) and as being "lord even of the sabbath." (2:28)

What is of concern to us here is the use of the title in connection with the parousia. We saw above Mark's description of that final day: "Then they will see 'the Son of Man coming in clouds' with great power and glory." (13:26) Jesus speaks also of the Son of Man coming "in the glory of his Father with the holy angels." (8:38) The crucial use of the title is found in the final confrontation when the high priest challenges Jesus, "Are you the Messiah, the Son of the Blessed One?"... "I am; and 'you will see the Son of Man seated at the right hand of the Power,' and 'coming with the clouds of heaven.'" (14:61–62) Jesus' reply brings his condemnation: "Then the high priest tore his clothes and said, 'Why do we still need witnesses? You have heard his blasphemy! What is your decision?' [The whole council] condemned him as deserving death." (14:63–64) For acknowledging himself to be the apocalyptic figure of the parousia, Jesus pays with his life.

D. The Apocalyptic Community

Christian communities living in expectation of the parousia have been present more or less continuously throughout the past nineteen hundred years. At times their behavior can be bizarre. For instance, convinced that the world is about to end, they will abandon their regular lives and simply wait for the climax of history. Such conduct may have been the object of Paul's admonition to the Thessalonians when he wrote them "to aspire to live quietly, to mind your own affairs, and to work with your hands, as we directed you, so that you may behave properly toward outsiders and be dependent on no one." (I Thessalonians 4:11–12)

Whether such aberrant behavior was present in Mark's church we do not know, but these Christians certainly had many reasons to believe the end was near. They would have understood the words that follow Mark's description of the parousia as being meant for them: "From the fig tree learn its lesson: as soon as its branch becomes tender and puts forth its leaves, you know that summer is near. So also, when you see these things taking place, you know that he is near, at the very gates. Truly I tell you, this generation will not pass away until all these things have taken place." (13:28–30)

At the same time the Gospel cautions against too precise an expectation: "But about that day or hour no one knows, neither the angels in heaven, nor the Son, but only the Father." (13:32) The caveat would have been aimed at those who, convinced the end was upon them, had acted precipitately, perhaps abandoning an orderly way of life. At the same time, one had to be vigilant: "Beware, keep alert; for you do not know when the time will come." (13:33)

The passage closes with an example the Gospel's readers would appreciate. Mark calls on his community to be like a well-run Roman household: "It is like a man going on a journey, when he leaves home and puts his slaves in charge, each with his work, and commands the doorkeeper to be on the watch. Therefore, keep awake—for you do not know when the master of the house will come, in the evening, or at midnight, or at cockcrow, or at dawn, or else he may find you asleep when he comes suddenly. And what I say to you I say to all: Keep awake." (13:34–37) A crucial figure in such a house was the doorkeeper (janitor) who had always to be ready to admit the owner on his return. Everyone is to stick to his task, yet remain always alert.

The readers of Mark and Mark himself went about their daily lives in the anticipation that the world around them would soon dissolve in a cosmic cataclysm. The empire which seemed all-powerful and indestructible was coming to an end. The pagan society with its plethora of gods and goddesses, its temples and sacrifices and its mystery cults, was about to be replaced by something entirely new, something called "the kingdom of God." It is this expectation that lies behind "the good news of Jesus Christ, the Son of God." (1:1)

STUDY QUESTIONS

1. What made 69 C.E. a significant year for the Roman Empire?
2. What was the Jewish reaction to the destruction of Jerusalem and its great temple?
3. Why might the disaster of 70 C.E. have been particularly traumatic for Mark's Christians?
4. What is the "parousia"?
5. What are the roots of the parousia in the Jewish traditions?
6. How are the changing expectations of early Christians reflected in the letters of Paul?
7. What appears to be the expectations of Mark's community?
8. What was meant by the "desolating sacrilege" mentioned in the first Gospel?
9. How does the first Gospel describe the parousia?
10. What are the sources of such a vision?
11. What two central themes of Mark's Gospel are linked in the title "Son of Man"?
12. What cautions does the first Gospel extend to its readers?

Chapter Seven

CHRIST AND SON OF GOD

I. THE CHRIST

A. *The Jewish Tradition*

The roots of Jesus' title, Christ,[1] lie deep in Jewish history. To symbolize the designation of David as king of Israel an ancient mideastern custom was followed: "Then Samuel took the horn of oil, and anointed him in the presence of his brothers; and the spirit of the LORD came mightily upon David from that day forward." (I Samuel 16:13). The reigns of David and of his son, Solomon, are still regarded as the golden age of Israel's history. When the exiles returned from Babylon in 539 B.C.E. it was at first their hope that an actual descendant of David might sit on the throne as an "anointed" ruler. "The days are surely coming, says the LORD, when I will raise up for David a righteous branch, and he shall reign as king and deal wisely, and shall execute justice and righteousness in the land." (Jeremiah 23:5)

Later that expectation could no longer be fulfilled since no descendants of David had survived. A hope then arose for a "messianic" figure who would come to restore glory to Israel. Yet, as Fredriksen observes: "The idea of the messiah, or, to use the Greek term, the Christ, does not figure overmuch in Biblical Judaism: it was a preoccupation of politically and religiously turbulent Judaism of the intertestamental[2] period, the Judaism of the Pharisees, Sadducees, and zealots...." (*Op. cit.* p. 34)

The first Christians believed Jesus of Nazareth to be the expected Messiah.[3] Being still part of the Jewish community, they would have shared their co–religionists' hope for the restoration of Israel's glory. Later, when Gentiles were being received into the Christian communi-

78

ties without accepting Judaism as well, the role of the Messiah underwent a change. This brings us to the apostle Paul.

B. In Paul

We are told in the Acts of the Apostles that "it was in Antioch that the disciples were first called 'Christians.'" (11:26) It was in that city that the first major Christian community was founded after Jerusalem. It may also have been where Gentiles first became followers of Jesus in large numbers. Paul himself came to Antioch after his conversion and left from there on his missionary journeys. Paul's usual reference to Jesus is as "Jesus Christ" or "Christ Jesus."

As the founder of largely Gentile communities, Paul makes clear that the messianic role of Jesus extends beyond the expectations of Israel: "There is no longer Jew or Greek, there is no longer slave or free, there is no longer male and female; for all of you are one in Christ Jesus." (Galatians 3:28) The apostle's wider vision of the messianic mission brought him into conflict not only with the Jews but with other Christians as well. Directly or indirectly, it was the Pauline understanding of the Messiah that had reached Mark's church.

C. In Mark

1. POLITICAL MESSIANISM

In sharp contrast to the apostle, Mark uses the title, "Christ/ Messiah" only seven times and just four times in reference to Jesus. The reason may lie in the fact that messianic claimants had been particularly troublesome in Palestine before and during the Jewish war. Many Jews, particularly the Zealots, saw the advent of the Messiah as God's signal to rise up in revolt against the oppression of the empire. Josephus cites several incidents of this sort. (*Op. cit.* pp. 147–48). Particularly infamous in this regard was Simon bar Giora. His revolutionary forces inflicted serious damage to the Roman forces in Palestine. He was captured at the end of the Jewish war, paraded through Rome as part of Titus' triumph, and executed in the Forum. Members of Mark's community would have been witnesses to his fate and have understood the evangelist's warning that we saw above: "False messiahs and false prophets will appear and produce signs and omens, to lead astray, if possible, the elect." (13:22)

In the light of the above, Mark and his community would have had to be very cautious in giving the title of Messiah to Jesus. Moreover, the readers of the first Gospel would have been painfully aware that the founder of Christianity had been executed by a Roman official as a royal claimant: "The inscription of the charge against [Jesus] read: 'The King of the Jews.'" (15:26) The Romans would have seen such a claim to be insurrectionist. Added to that was the manner of Jesus' execution, the usual fate of revolutionaries.[4] Yet Mark cannot deny that Jesus of Nazareth was acknowledged by his earliest followers to be the expected Messiah. What the first evangelist does is to stress the purely religious nature of Jesus' mission. As Fredriksen observes: "Mark, in fact, claims messianic status for Jesus by emptying the concept of any political content...." (*Op. cit.* p. 50)

At one point, Mark seeks to sever the connection between the Messiah and the Davidic lineage: "While Jesus was teaching in the temple, he said, 'How can the scribes say that the Messiah is the son of David? David himself, by the Holy Spirit, declared, "The Lord said to my Lord, 'Sit at my right hand, until I put your enemies under your feet.'" David himself calls him Lord; so how can he be his son?' And the large crowd was listening to him with delight." (12:35–37) If the Messiah is not a descendant of David, then the messianic title is not necessarily a claim to regal status.

In the relating of Jesus' appearance before Pontius Pilate the first Gospel seeks again to defuse the charge of Jesus having actually been a claimant to the throne of Israel. When Pontius Pilate asks Jesus, "Are you the King of the Jews?" (15:2) his answer, "You say so," is ambiguous at best. The procurator himself doubts the validity of the charge against Jesus. "[Pilate] realized that it was out of jealousy that the chief priests had handed [Jesus] over." (15:10) Mark was powerless to repudiate the accusation but he does his best to undermine it.

One also wonders if the mocking of Jesus by his guards was not Mark's way of making ridiculous the notion that Jesus was of royal descent. "Then the soldiers led him into the courtyard of the palace (that is, the governor's headquarters); and they called together the whole cohort. And they clothed him in a purple cloak; and after twisting some thorns into a crown, they put it on him. And they began saluting him, 'Hail, King of the Jews!' They struck his head with a reed, spat upon him, and knelt down in homage to him." (15:16–19) The scene of Jesus in the "royal purple," crowned with thorns and abused by his "subjects," would emphasize how ridiculous was the picture of Jesus as a king.

2. THE TRUE MESSIAH

By freeing Jesus from any claim to royal descent Mark would have freed the Christians from any taint of revolutionary intent. Yet Jesus was the Messiah. Mark's view is seen at a crucial moment in the Gospel: "Jesus went with his disciples to the villages of Caesarea Philippi;[5] and on the way he asked his disciples, 'Who do people say that I am?' And they answered him, 'John the Baptist'; and others, 'Elijah'; and still others, 'one of the prophets.' He asked them, 'But who do you say that I am?' Peter answered him, 'You are the Messiah.'" (8:27–29) Though Jesus does not directly accept the title at this point, he does join the designation of Messiah with that of "the Son of Man."

As we saw in the previous chapter, the latter title is that of a suffering savior: "The Son of Man must undergo great suffering, and be rejected by the elders, the chief priests, and the scribes, and be killed, and after three days rise again." (8:31; see also 9:31; 10:33) The transformation of the Messiah from a regal, triumphant figure to one who suffers, particularly one who undergoes so degrading a fate as crucifixion, was indeed radical. As Raymond Brown notes: "Jews who did not accept Christian claims might well point out that a Messiah whose life terminated in suffering was a drastic change of the concept of the expected anointed Davidic king." (*NJBC*, p. 1358a)

When Peter protests the notion of a suffering Messiah he is given a severe rebuke: "Get behind me, Satan! For you are setting your mind not on divine things but on human things." (8:31) Were there Christians who still expected the return of a triumphant Messiah? If so, the Gospel reminds the reader that a time of testing lies ahead: "If any want to become my followers, let them deny themselves and take up their cross and follow me. For those who want to save their life will lose it, and those who lose their life for my sake, and for the sake of the gospel, will save it." (8:34–35) Not only Jesus, but the Good News itself will demand sacrifices of the believer.

3. THE MESSIANIC SECRET

When Peter responds to Jesus, "You are the Messiah," (8:29) Mark notes, "[Jesus] sternly ordered them not to tell anyone about him." (8:30) Jesus' attempt to conceal his curing of illnesses (1:44; 5:43; 7:36) may be part of an additional precaution Mark took to show that Jesus strove to hide his identity during his public life. Such an effort would have served a purpose of Mark's. If Jesus made no claims to be the "Christ" during his lifetime and prevented others from doing so, then a charge that he had fomented trouble in Palestine loses its cogency. When Jesus does admit that he is the Messiah (14:61–62), it is as a prisoner of the temple leaders and at a time when he appears the least messianic.

However, any ambiguity about Jesus claiming to be the Messiah is cleared up by Mark when Jesus is confronted by the high priest: " 'Are you the Messiah, the Son of the Blessed One?'[6] Jesus said, 'I am; and "you will see the Son of Man seated at the right hand of the Power," and "coming with the clouds of heaven." ' " (15:61–62) Jesus not only embraces the title of Messiah, but he joins it with that of the Son of God. We now turn to the meaning that title had for Mark's readers.

II. SON OF GOD

A. *In the Hebrew Bible*

In origin, the people of Israel were monolatrous, that is, they did not deny the existence of other gods, but worshiped only their God, "Yahweh," whom they believed was superior to his rival gods. "Who is like you, O LORD, among the gods? Who is like you, majestic in holiness, awesome in splendor, doing wonders?" (Exodus 15:11) "God has taken his place in the divine council; in the midst of the gods he holds judgment." (Psalm 82:1) In time, the Jews came to the realization that there was only one God: "I am God, and there is no other." (Isaiah 46:9) The Jews' refusal to compromise their monotheism by any form of syncretism brought them great pain and suffering. The second book of Maccabees is eloquent testimony to their faithfulness to Yahweh, the one God.

By the first century C.E., the Jewish understanding of the "oneness" of God was so rigid that they would not tolerate any hint of divinity in any other creature. We can get some feeling for the intensity of their absolute monotheism from an incident reported by Josephus. It seems that Emperor Caligula, who had declared himself divine, ordered his general, Petronius, to erect a statue of the emperor in Jerusalem's temple. The following was the result: "The Jews with their wives and children massed on the plain near the city...they were ready to offer themselves as victims with their wives and children. Such a reply filled Petronius with wonder and pity for the unparalleled religious fervor of the brave men and the courage that made them ready to die." (*Op. cit.* pp. 140–141)

It is against this background that we must evaluate those spoken of as "sons" of God in the Hebrew Bible: "Thus says the LORD: Israel is my firstborn son." (Exodus 4:22) "When Israel was a child, I loved him, and out of Egypt I called my son." (Hosea 11:1) David is also depicted as a "son of God": "You are my son; today I have begotten you." (Psalm 2:7) "I will make him the firstborn." (Psalm 89:27) In this connection Joseph A. Fitzmyer observes: "The dominant idea underlying the use of 'Son of God' in the Jewish world was that of divine election for a God-given task and the corresponding obedience to such a vocation." (*NJBC*, p. 1393b) Among the Jews of the first century C.E. there could be no hint of divinity in the title "Son of God."

B. In Paul

In his authentic letters, Paul refers to Jesus as the "Son of God" or as God's "Son" ten times. Writing around 54 C.E. to the Galatians, the apostle says, "I live by faith in the Son of God, who loved me and gave himself for me." (2:20; see also 4:4,6) There are similar affirmations in I Corinthians (1:9; 15:28), II Corinthians (1:19) and in Romans (1:9; 5:10; 8:3). The most significant affirmation is at the beginning of Paul's letter to the Romans when he speaks of "the gospel concerning his Son, who was descended from David according to the flesh and was declared to be Son of God with power according to the spirit of holiness by resurrection from the dead, Jesus Christ our Lord." (1:1–4) This would seem to indicate a radical transformation in the status of Jesus upon his resurrection.

We have something similar in Paul's letter to the Philippians: "Let the same mind be in you that was in Christ Jesus—

> Who, though he was in the form of God,
> did not regard equality with God as something to be exploited,
> But emptied himself, taking the form of a slave,
> being born in human likeness.
> And being found in human form,
> he humbled himself and became obedient to the point of death—
> even death on a cross.
> Therefore God also highly exalted him
> and gave him the name that is above every name,
> So that at the name of Jesus every knee should bend,
> in heaven and on earth and under the earth,
> And every tongue should confess that Jesus Christ is Lord,
> to the glory of God the Father." (2:5–11)[7]

The "name of Jesus" at which "every knee should bend" is that of "Lord." The word in Greek is *Kyrios*, meaning "Master." In Paul, "Lord Jesus Christ" and "Jesus Christ our Lord" appear some forty times. It is a title that has more significance than it might seem at first.

In reading from the Hebrew Bible the custom arose of substituting for the name of God, *YHWH*, the word for "Master," *Adonai*. The custom continues among Jews today. When the Septuagint translation was made the Greek *Kyrios* replaced *YHWH*. Thus when Paul speaks of Jesus as "Lord" he means to accord to Jesus some share in the divinity of God himself. Nevertheless, we should remember that it will be some three centuries before the church will develop a more theological expression of Jesus' participation in the divine nature.

C. In Mark

1. THE BAPTIZER

The author of the first Gospel never refers to Jesus as "Lord" in the way Paul does, probably because the above Jewish custom was unknown to his Gentile readership. On the other hand, the opening line of Mark is: "The beginning of the good news of Jesus Christ, the Son of God." (1:1) The meaning of "the Son of God" for Mark is then made clear in the opening scene of the Gospel. The central figure of that scene is the one known as "John the Baptizer." (1:4; 16:14,24)

Josephus has the following passage: "Herod had [John surnamed the Baptist] put to death, though he was a good man and had exhorted the Jews to live righteous lives, to practice justice toward their fellows and piety toward God.... Herod became alarmed. Eloquence that had so great an effect on mankind might lead to some form of sedition.... John, because of Herod's suspicions, was brought in chains to Machere us... and there put to death." (*Jewish Antiquities*, 18:116–119) Later in the Gospel, Mark recounts another version of how John met his fate (6:17–29)[8]

Mark also reports that there were those who said of Jesus, "John the Baptizer has been raised from the dead; and for this reason these powers are at work in [Jesus]." (6:14) When Jesus asks his disciples, "Who do people say that I am?" they answered, "John the Baptist...." (8:28) Like Jesus, John apparently had disciples who survived him and attempted to carry out his mission. Mark mentions them: "Now John's disciples and the Pharisees were fasting; and people came and said to him, 'Why do John's disciples and the disciples of the Pharisees fast, but your disciples do not fast?'" (2:18)[9]

As described by Mark, the Baptizer is an impressive figure: "John the Baptizer appeared in the wilderness, proclaiming a baptism of repentance for the forgiveness of sins. And people from the whole Judean countryside and all the people of Jerusalem were going out to him, and were baptized by him in the river Jordan, confessing their sins. Now John was clothed with camel's hair, with a leather belt around his waist, and he ate locusts and wild honey." (1:4–6) John resembles what II Kings tells us about Elijah, the desert prophet, as "a hairy man, with a leather belt around his waist." (1:8)

In many ways for Mark, John is a bridge between the Jewish traditions and Christianity. He is the fulfillment of an Isaian prophecy: "As it is written in the prophet Isaiah, 'See, I am sending my messenger ahead of you, who will prepare your way; the voice of one crying out in the wilderness: "Prepare the way of the Lord, make his paths straight."' "

(Mark 1:2–3) The quotation is actually a combination of Malachi: "See, I am sending my messenger to prepare the way before me," (3:1) and of Isaiah: "A voice cries out: 'In the wilderness prepare the way of the LORD, make straight in the desert a highway for our God.'" (40:3)

Mark's community must have known of Jesus' baptism by John. Given the undoubted prestige of the Baptizer, that fact must have been embarrassing. There may have been those who felt that John actually had a better claim to the title of Messiah. Yet, no matter the fame of John the Baptizer, Mark emphasizes that he was subordinate to Jesus. As John himself says: "The one who is more powerful than I is coming after me; I am not worthy to stoop down and untie the thong of his sandals." (1:7)

2. THE BAPTISM

Having made it clear that the Baptizer prepared the way for Jesus' coming, Mark introduces the Nazorean to his readers: "In those days Jesus came from Nazareth of Galilee and was baptized by John in the Jordan. And just as he was coming up out of the water, he saw the heavens torn apart and the Spirit descending like a dove[10] on him. And a voice came from heaven, 'You are my Son, the Beloved; with you I am well pleased.'" (1:9–11) The vision and the voice are for Jesus alone. It is here that he is informed of his identity as the Son of God.

The nuance is important. Earlier, in the letter to the Romans, Paul stated that Jesus "was declared to be Son of God with power according to the spirit of holiness by resurrection from the dead...." (1:4) Later, in the Gospels of Matthew (1:20) and Luke (1:32), the identity of Jesus is revealed to Joseph and Mary at his conception. By contrast, in Mark only Jesus really knows his own identity at first. True, the evil spirits know, but Jesus silences them. "Whenever the unclean spirits saw him, they fell down before him and shouted, 'You are the Son of God!' But he sternly ordered them not to make him known." (3:11–12)

3. THE TRANSFIGURATION

Later, what is told to Jesus at his baptism is announced to the leaders of Jesus' disciples. "Jesus took with him Peter and James and John, and led them up a high mountain apart, by themselves. And he was transfigured before them, and his clothes became dazzling white, such as no one on earth could bleach them. And there appeared to them Elijah with Moses, who were talking with Jesus." (9:2–4) The symbolism is impressive; the law (Moses) and the prophets (Elijah) give testimony to the role of Jesus. As he did with John the Baptizer, Mark makes clear to his readers that the Jewish traditions point to Jesus as the one who is to come.

But there is a greater testimony to be made: "Then a cloud overshadowed them, and from the cloud there came a voice, 'This is my Son, the Beloved; listen to him!'" (9:7) The scene is reminiscent of Moses' mountain-top encounter with Yahweh on Mount Sinai: "Then the LORD said to Moses, 'I am going to come to you in a dense cloud, in order that the people may hear when I speak with you and so trust you ever after.'" (Exodus 19:9) The three principal followers of Jesus have been informed with the greatest solemnity of Jesus' identity and admonished to be silent on the matter "until after the Son of Man had risen from the dead." (9.9)

We are told that they complied: "So they kept the matter to themselves, questioning what this rising from the dead could mean." (9:10) Again, the apostles fail to understand what Jesus is saying. We can conclude that the solemn declaration of Jesus' identity was more for Mark's fellow believers than for the immediate witnesses.

There is another testimony to Jesus' relationship to God found in the first Gospel. It comes when Jesus is alone, facing his final ordeal. In the garden of Gethsemani, Jesus himself addresses God with the intimacy of a true Son. He prays "Abba, Father." (14:36) "Abba" is Aramaic for the familiar address of child to father, something of a parallel to our "daddy." For Mark, the paternal relationship between Jesus and his divine Father is most intimate.

4. THE CENTURION

As we saw earlier, there is one person in the first Gospel who knows who Jesus really is: "Now when the centurion, who stood facing him, saw that in this way he breathed his last, he said, 'Truly this man was God's Son!'" (15:39) It is a Gentile who makes the essential act of faith. He does so when Jesus appears the least divine, a mangled figure on a cross. The real challenge for Mark's Gentile Christians was not a suffering Messiah, but a divinity who suffered as a human being. We have now come to a central theme of Mark, the relationship between the human and the divine in Jesus.

STUDY QUESTIONS

1. What is the Messiah in Jewish traditions?
2. In what way did the apostle Paul expand the earlier meaning of Messiah?
3. Why does the Gospel of Mark use the title "Christ" more sparingly?
4. Why was the accusation that Jesus claimed to be "King of the Jews" particularly troubling to Mark's community?
5. What reason might Mark's Gospel have had for linking the Messiah and the Son of Man in Jesus?
6. What was the "Messianic secret"?
7. Is there any background for the title "Son of God" in the Jewish traditions?
8. Is there any reference in the letters of Paul to Jesus' divinity?
9. Does the first Gospel reflect a belief in Jesus' divinity?
10. On what two occasions does God acknowledge Jesus as his Son?
11. What is the meaning of "Abba"?

Chapter Eight

DIVINE AND YET HUMAN

I. INTRODUCTION

Mark's community was still centuries away from the philosophical and theological expression of Jesus' humanity and divinity we share today. There were to be years of painful struggle between those who sought to preserve Jesus' divinity by limiting his humanity and those who tried to preserve his humanity by making him somehow less divine. The roots of the struggle lay in the heritage of Christianity itself. On the one hand were the Jewish Christians with their strict monotheism and, on the other, were the Gentile Christians with their polytheistic background. Only after centuries would the church be able to accomplish a resolution of the conflict. Such was the achievement of the ecumenical councils in Nicaea (325 C.E.), Ephesus (431 C.E.), and Chalcedon (451 C.E.).

II. MARK'S CHALLENGE

As they were Gentiles, Mark's Christians had been previously involved in one or more of the polytheistic sects that made up most of the empire's religions including the Roman state religion. Speaking of such Gentiles in general, Robin Lane Fox observes, "Through myth and Homeric poetry, the visits of the gods continued to draw on a deep reserve of potential experience which poets and artists could exploit but which most people did not exclude from life's possibilities." (*Pagans and Christians*, p. 122) What was true for the Greco-Roman Pantheon was also true for the newer cults: "In the mystery religions, too, the old patterns of a god's appearance were not displaced. There was an idea that gods might appear especially to people who had been initiated and would help them in their subsequent crises." (*Op. cit.* pp.

89

124–125) Moreover, the emperors from Julius Caesar to Nero were regarded as divine. Divine beings making appearances in human form would not have been a strange notion to the Gentiles of Mark's time.

Then there is the incident in Acts where Paul and his companion Barnabas are taken to be gods. "When the crowds saw what Paul had done, they shouted in the Lycaonian language, 'The gods have come down to us in human form!' Barnabas they called Zeus, and Paul they called Hermes, because he was the chief speaker. The priest of Zeus, whose temple was just outside the city, brought oxen and garlands to the gates; he and the crowds wanted to offer sacrifice." (14:11–13) In summing up, Fox quotes an earlier study, "What is clear…is that Christianity came into a world tantalized by a belief that some men had seen God." (*Op. cit.* p. 165)

As we saw in the previous chapter, the first Gospel presents Jesus as the Son of God. It is solemnly announced at the baptism and transfiguration, testified to by the evil spirits, claimed by Jesus himself, and finally professed by that crucial figure, the centurion at the foot of the cross. Mark's readers accepted Jesus as a divinity, but was he simply one appearing in human form? Again, speaking of the Gentiles, Fox notes: "There was no end to the gods' human disguises, as old men and women, heralds and, frequently, young and beautiful people.…" (Fox, *op. cit.* p. 106) Was Jesus a god in human disguise?

III. MARK'S RESPONSE

A. *The Galilean*

To counteract the affirmative response, Mark takes a number of steps to emphasize the reality of Jesus' humanity. If it is correct, as we noted above, that Jesus himself only learned of his relationship to God at his baptism, then up to that time Jesus was unaware of his divinity and would have regarded himself as an ordinary human being. His family apparently shared the same opinion. After all, if anyone would suspect that there was something extraordinary about Jesus it would be a member of his family. Yet when Jesus had gained a great deal of notoriety and these reports reached his family, Mark tells the reader: "When his family heard it, they went out to restrain him, for people were saying, 'He has gone out of his mind.'" (3:21) They understandably tried to bring him back to Nazareth. (3:31)

And what of Jesus' lifelong friends and acquaintances in Nazareth? Did they find him in any way extraordinary? Mark makes it clear they did not.

> [Jesus] came to his hometown.... On the sabbath he began to teach in the synagogue, and many who heard him were astounded. They said, "Where did this man get all this? What is this wisdom that has been given to him? What deeds of power are being done by his hands! Is not this the carpenter,[1] the son of Mary and brother of James and Joses and Judas and Simon, and are not his sisters[2] here with us?" And they took offense at him. (6:2–3)

Apparently, these villagers who had been Jesus' friends and acquaintances for all but the last years of his life could not accept Jesus as anything but the local woodworker. They even found offensive the claims that he was something more. In Mark, Jesus, prior to the beginning of his public life, is seen as a quite ordinary human being.

B. The Public Man

1. LIMITATIONS

However, Jesus was anything but ordinary after his baptism. He had become a wonderworker of great power. Yet Mark still shows us someone with human limitations. We have the incident of the woman suffering from hemorrhages for twelve years. She seeks only to touch Jesus' cloak and, on doing so, is cured. "Immediately aware that power had gone forth from him, Jesus turned about in the crowd and said, 'Who touched my clothes?' And his disciples said to him, 'You see the crowd pressing in on you; how can you say, 'Who touched me?'" (5:30–31) Like any other human being, Jesus was unable to determine who had bumped against him in the crowd.

Healers were known to Mark's readers. They usually attempted to cure by use of rituals. The description the first Gospel gives of a deaf mute's cure by Jesus would have sounded familiar: "[Jesus] took him aside in private, away from the crowd, and put his fingers into his ears, and he spat and touched his tongue. Then looking up to heaven, he

sighed and said to him, 'Ephphatha,' that is, 'Be opened.' And immediately his ears were opened, his tongue was released, and he spoke
plainly." (7:33–35) Even in doing something extraordinary, Mark man-
ages to make Jesus appear ordinary.

The point is made even more forcibly later on. "[Jesus] took the
blind man by the hand and led him out of the village; and when he had
put saliva on his eyes and laid his hands on him, he asked him, 'Can
you see anything?' And the man looked up and said, 'I can see people,
but they look like trees, walking.' Then Jesus laid his hands on his eyes
again; and he looked intently and his sight was restored, and he saw
everything clearly." (8:23–25) Not only did Jesus use a ritual but the
cure itself was gradual rather than instantaneous.

Suetonius (*The Twelve Caesars*, p. 284) reports the cure of a blind
man by Emperor Vespasian. The cure was effected by spitting on the
man's eyes. Vespasian was ruling the empire when Mark was writing. The incident could have been common knowledge. If so, then
Jesus' cure of the blind man was not outside the range of human
achievement. Again the humanity of Jesus is not overshadowed by
his wonderworking.

2. HUMAN EMOTIONS

To display emotions does not as such militate against divinity. The
Hebrew Bible attributes to Yahweh anger, love, pity, and the like.
Similar emotions were ascribed by the Romans to their gods. Yet, fun-
damentally, emotions are characteristically human and Mark frequently mentions Jesus' emotional responses. Jesus takes pity on a leper.
(1:41) When the Pharisees were prepared to condemn Jesus for curing
on the sabbath, "[Jesus] looked around at them with anger; he was
grieved at their hardness of heart...." (3:5) Again frustrated with the
Pharisees, Jesus "sighed deeply in his spirit." (8:12)

Jesus is also disappointed by the dullness of his disciples: "Do you
still not perceive or understand? Are your hearts hardened?" (8:17)
When his disciples, with the best of intentions, sought to prevent children from approaching, and "Jesus saw this, he was indignant."
(10:14) We have already commented on the limitations of Jesus' followers as Mark depicts them. The Gospel's readers could assume that
Jesus expressed his frustration more than once.

Particularly touching was the occasion when a man approached Jesus. On learning that the man had lived a remarkably virtuous life, "Jesus, looking at him, loved him...." (10:21) Mark leaves to the reader's imagination the disappointment of Jesus when the same man, unable to make the sacrifices demanded of Jesus' disciples, "went away grieving...." (10:22) These touches, though few in number, still remind the reader of Jesus' underlying humanity.

3. THE PASSION

It is in his suffering and death that Mark's Jesus appears the most human. Actually, suffering and dying gods were known to Mark's readers. Even if they had not themselves been in a mystery cult they would have been aware of such deities. Dionysus (Bacchus to the Romans) was torn apart; Osirus was murdered and also dismembered; Attis, the consort of Cybele, was a suicide. Though their stories have anthropomorphic elements, none of these figures was regarded as human. In recounting Jesus' final hours, Mark never lets the reader forget his profound humanity.

As the time of his suffering approaches, Jesus, aware of what he is about to face, shrinks from his fate. In the garden of Gethsemani, he tells his disciples, "I am deeply grieved, even to death; remain here, and keep awake." And going a little farther, he throws himself on the ground and prays that, if it might be, he could be spared his fate. He says, "Abba, Father, for you all things are possible; remove this cup from me; yet, not what I want, but what you want." (14:34–36) The scene is made all the more poignant by Jesus' use of the Aramaic diminutive "Abba," such as a child might address his father, a particularly humanizing touch.

Mark does not spare the reader in recounting the passion and death of Jesus. Jesus is unresisting in the hands of his enemies. He is mocked, beaten, spat upon, insulted, and crowned with thorns before being led out of the city to the place of punishment. There he is crucified between two common criminals, a manner of execution reserved for slaves and non-citizens. During the hours of his agony on the cross, Jesus is mocked by his enemies, the passersby, and even those crucified with him.

Our vision of Jesus on the cross is usually sanitized. This was not the case for Mark's readers. There was ample opportunity for them to see an unfortunate wretch, already flogged, burdened with the cross-beam on which he will be hung, driven through the streets to a city gate, there to hang in agony until released by death.[3] Crucifixion was a particularly ugly and degrading way to die. For the pagan Romans the very notion of a divine being hanging on a cross would have been bizarre to say the least.

In fact, it was of an embarrassment to Christians. We mentioned earlier a second century Roman *graffitus* crudely depicting a crucified figure with a donkey's head, captioned "Alexamenous worships his god," obviously a mockery of the Christian faith. Actually, the cross was not used as a Christian symbol until late in the fourth century when that mode of punishment had been abandoned.

Besides having no doubt witnessed crucifixions themselves, there may actually have been a living link between Mark's community and the final suffering of Jesus. Mark mentions one "Simon of Cyrene, the father of Alexander and Rufus" (15:21), who was forced to come to Jesus' aid. We can assume that Alexander and Rufus were known to the evangelist's community. A Rufus is mentioned by Paul when he writes to Rome (16:13). If so, Mark's community would have had to deal with a very vivid recounting of Jesus' death on a cross.

In fact, so human does Jesus appear as his life ends that the faith of Mark's readers in Jesus' divinity must have been challenged. In this context we can seen the crucial role played by the centurion in the first Gospel. "Now when the centurion, who stood facing him, saw that in this way he breathed his last, he said, 'Truly this man was God's Son!'" (15:39) Here was a man who had seen none of Jesus' wondrous deeds. The only words he heard were an apparent cry of despair uttered from the cross. "*Eloi, Eloi, lema sabachthani?*" (15:34), meaning, "My God, my God, why have you forsaken me?" Yet this Gentile recognizes the divinity of Jesus.

C. The Roman

Every culture has an ideal, an image reflecting the characteristic outlook of a people. R. B. Barrow in his book, *The Romans*, observes:

Throughout their history the Romans were acutely aware that there is "power" outside man, individually or collectively, of which man must take account. He must subordinate himself to something. If he refuses, he invites disaster.... Willing cooperation gives a sense of dedication ... at a higher level he becomes conscious of a vocation, of a mission for himself.... From the earliest days of Rome we can detect in the Roman a sense of dedication.... This is the clue to Roman character and to Roman history." (pp. 9–10)

As was pointed out, most of Mark's community were not originally Roman. However, it is often the immigrant who seeks most zealously to emulate his new country's ideals. In this case, that ideal had its roots in the philosophy of the Stoic. To give two examples of this outlook: "Good men are not dragged by Fate; they follow it and keep in step.... I am not being forced into anything and I am not putting up with anything against my will. I do not submit to God, I agree with him...." (Seneca the Younger, *An Essay about Providence* 5.4,6); "I have submitted my freedom of choice unto God." (Epictetus, quoted in Michael Grant, *The World of Rome*, p. 227)

There is much in Mark's Jesus that reflects the Stoic vision. Jesus is completely "conscious of a vocation, of a mission for himself." He cannot be deterred from carrying it out. On the morning following his initial success in Capernaum, Jesus is alone, at prayer, outside the city when his disciples, led by Simon (Peter), come urging him to capitalize on his achievement: "Everyone is searching for you." (1:37) But Jesus' mission is not to a single locale: " 'Let us go on to the neighboring towns, so that I may proclaim the message there also; for that is what I came out to do.' And he went throughout Galilee, proclaiming the message in their synagogues and casting out demons." (1:38–39) Jesus is overwhelmingly a man with a mission.

Fredriksen notes: "Mark's Jesus is a man in a hurry, dashing throughout Galilee in rapid, almost random motion, from synagogue to invalid, from shore to grain field to sea, casting out demons and amazing those who witness him. The spare prose and staccato cures create a mood of nervous anticipation." (*Op. cit.* p. 44) Though Jesus' peregrinations as recounted by Mark appear random, there is an inevitable destination. "[Jesus] took the twelve aside again and began to tell them what was to happen to him, saying, 'See, we are going up to Jerusalem, and the Son of Man will be handed over to the chief priests and the scribes, and they will condemn him to death; then they will hand him over to the Gentiles; they will mock him, and spit upon him, and flog him, and kill him....'" (10:32–34) Jesus, always aware of his fate, could say as the true Stoic, "I am not being forced into anything and I am not putting up with anything against my will. I do not submit to God, I agree with him...." (Seneca the Younger, *op. cit.* 5.6)

When Peter, on hearing Jesus describe his fate, protests, he is rebuked by Jesus in no uncertain terms, "Get behind me, Satan! For you are setting your mind not on divine things but on human things." (8:32) When Jesus is informed that his family, including his mother, have come to fetch him, his response is " 'Who are my mother and my brothers?' And looking at those who sat around him, he said, 'Here are my mother and my brothers! Whoever does the will of God is my brother and sister and mother.'" (3:32–35) Jesus demands of Mark's readers the same dedication to the will of God: "If any want to become my followers, let them deny themselves and take up their cross and follow me." (8:34) For those readers, as we have seen, the "cross" had a very vivid and ugly meaning.

The tradition of a Roman Jesus persisted. The first artistic rendition we have of Jesus, a second century statuette, shows him as a curly haired, beardless young man clad in a tunic, much the typical Roman. Could this have been how Mark's community would have imagined Jesus? Whatever is the truth, Mark certainly gave his readers a vivid picture of a very human Jesus who was, for the believer, the Son of God.

IV. THE AFTERMATH

A. *Matthew and Luke*

It helps in appreciating Mark's depiction of Jesus to see how the succeeding evangelists portray him. Some twenty or so years later the Gospels of Matthew and Luke appeared, both influenced by the earlier Mark. Both agree with their predecessor that Jesus is a divine being. In Matthew, it is Joseph who is so informed (1:20), and in Luke it is Mary

(1:32). However, Matthew and Luke are both more circumspect than Mark when it comes to Jesus' humanity.

Matthew and Luke seem reluctant to attribute emotion to Jesus. For instance, we are told in Mark, "[Jesus] looked around at them with anger; he was grieved at their hardness of heart...." (3:5) Matthew and Luke make no such comment in their parallel passages (Matthew 12:13; Luke 6:10). Similarly, when Mark tells the reader that Jesus was indignant that his disciples barred children from coming to him (10:14), Matthew and Luke make no mention of Jesus' indignation (Matthew 19:14; Luke 18:16). When, in Mark, the good man comes to Jesus we are told that "Jesus, looking at him, loved him." (10:21) The two later Gospels omit the expression of emotion (Matthew 19:21; Luke 18:22).

Other indications of a toning down in expressing Jesus' humanity in Matthew and Luke are that both eliminate Jesus' use of the diminutive for "Father," "Abba," found in Mark (Matthew 26:39; Luke 22:42). Where Mark tells the reader that Jesus' family "went out to restrain him, for people were saying, 'He has gone out of his mind'" (3:21), neither of the other two Gospels has a parallel passage. Neither evangelist has passages that parallel Mark's stories of the cures of the deaf mute and the blind man (7:31–35; 8:23–25). Recall that in these cures Jesus used rituals involving the use of saliva.

Both the later Gospels also have difficulty with Jesus' lack of knowledge. Matthew eliminates the reference to Jesus' being unaware of who touched him when the woman with the hemorrhage is cured (9:22). Luke omits the passage where Mark has, "But about that day or hour no one knows, neither the angels in heaven, nor the Son, but only the Father." (13:32)

Matthew is faithful in large measure to Mark's treatment of Jesus' suffering and death. Luke, perhaps more sensitive to Jesus' divinity, softens the picture. Jesus, for instance, is not overwhelmed with grief in Gethsemani (22:40–46 *vs.* Mark 14:34). When the servant's ear is cut off (Mark 14:47), Jesus, in Luke, immediately restores it (22:51).

Luke's most significant deviations from Mark come when Jesus is condemned by Pilate. Here Jesus is not scourged as in Mark (15:15), and Jesus' torment by the soldiers (Mark 15:16–20) is omitted. In

Luke, Jesus pauses on his way to Golgotha to comfort the weeping women (23:27–31), certainly dimming the picture of a suffering victim. At the place of crucifixion, Jesus is not derided by the passersby (Mark 15:29). Those present are passive, and only Jesus' avowed enemies mock him (23:35). However, for these Jesus has prayed: "Father, forgive them; for they do not know what they are doing." (23:34)

In Mark, both of the thieves crucified with Jesus join in the deriding of him (15:32). Here Luke makes a radical change. Only one thief taunts Jesus and is reprimanded by the other: "Do you not fear God, since you are under the same sentence of condemnation? And we indeed have been condemned justly, for we are getting what we deserve for our deeds, but this man has done nothing wrong." (23:40–41) To the "good" thief, Jesus promises, "Truly I tell you, today you will be with me in Paradise." (23:43) Jesus faces death assured of salvation. Thus it is not surprising that Luke omits the "*Eloi, Eloi, lema sabachthani ...*" of Mark (15:34). In Luke, Jesus' final words are, "Father, into your hands I commend my spirit." (23:46) The witnesses of this scene, Luke tells the reader, "returned home, beating their breasts." (23:48)

The stark depiction of Jesus' crucifixion in Mark has been softened by Luke. One might say that Luke allows more of the divinity to shine through. By analogy, Mark's crucifix is like those one sees in Latin countries, so realistic as to be repelling: every welt and gash runs with blood; the head is wreathed with the cruel crown of thorns and falls forward on the chest; the agonized death is fully apparent. Luke's crucifix is idealized and seems bathed in a glow; an almost unblemished figure gazes up into the heavens, with only a faint hint of the suffering Jesus endured.

B. John

When we come to the end of the first century and the composition of the fourth and final Gospel, the pendulum has swung further from Mark. In the first Gospel Jesus' divinity appears limited by his humanity. In John the reader is quickly disabused of any such conclusion. Jesus' baptism by John the Baptizer, found in the Synoptic Gospels (Mark 1:9; Matthew 3:13; Luke 3:21), is omitted. "A baptism of repentance for the forgiveness of sins" (Mark 1:4) would be too great a hint of human frailty for John.

John similarly treats any expression of ignorance on Jesus' part. Confronted with the hungry multitude, Jesus asks Philip: "Where are we to buy bread for these people to eat?" But John tells us, Jesus "said this to test him, for he himself knew what he was going to do." (6:5–6) When Jesus selects Judas as an apostle, it is with full knowledge that he will be the betrayer (6:70–71). Not even in praying could there be any doubt implied on the part of Jesus: "Father, I thank you for having heard me. I knew that you always hear me, but I have said this for the sake of the crowd standing here, so that they may believe that you sent me." (11:41–42)

When Jesus faces his coming passion and death, there is no faltering: "Now my soul is troubled. And what should I say—'Father, save me from this hour?' No, it is for this reason that I have come to this hour. 'Father, glorify your name.' Then a voice came from heaven, 'I have glorified it, and I will glorify it again.'" (12:27–28) However, Jesus makes it clear to those around him, "This voice has come for your sake, not for mine." (12:30) Nor does John's Jesus die a hapless, powerless victim: "I lay down my life in order to take it up again. No one takes it from me, but I lay it down of my own accord. I have power to lay it down, and I have power to take it up again." (10:17–18)

In John, when the mob comes to seize him, Jesus' power is made evident: "Then Jesus, knowing all that was to happen to him, came forward and asked them, 'Whom are you looking for?' They answered, 'Jesus of Nazareth.' Jesus replied, 'I am he.' ... When Jesus said to them, 'I am he,' they stepped back and fell to the ground." (18:4–6) As Raymond Brown says, "the evangelist defended the divinity of Jesus so massively that the Fourth Gospel scarcely allows for human limitation.... The entire presentation protects Jesus from whatever could be a challenge to divinity." (*The Churches the Apostles Left Behind*, p. 105) Where the first Gospel had to stress Jesus' humanity lest it be regarded as merely a disguise, the final Gospel had to downplay that same humanity to defend the belief that Jesus was divine.

Early in the second century, some members of John's community were troubled by the stress (overstress in their opinion) of Jesus' divinity at the expense of his humanity. Their view is reflected in the letters of John:[4] "By this you know the Spirit of God: every spirit that confesses that Jesus Christ has come in the flesh is from God...." (I John 4:2) Apparently the community split up, and not amicably: "Many deceivers have gone out into the world, those who do not confess that Jesus Christ has come in the flesh; any such person is the deceiver and the Antichrist!" (II John 7) The group that refused to modify their stress on Jesus' divinity came to be regarded as heretics by the main body of Christians whereas their opponents, along with the Gospel of John and the letters of John, were accepted as orthodox.

C. Continuing Tension

For the Christian communities that followed those of the first century the young, tunic-clad, curly-headed Jesus of the Romans became the severe, bearded, regally robed "Pancrator" of the Byzantines. Each era has had its own image of Jesus. Today, we have inherited our image from Renaissance art, a depiction often romanticized to the point of unreality. When such a picture of Jesus is challenged, as it is in Martin Scorsese's film, *The Last Temptation of Christ*, our reaction can be quite negative; the Jesus of the film seems all too human. So, in a way, we have come full circle. Like Mark's community we readily accept that Jesus is divine, but possibly at the cost of downplaying his humanity. The first Gospel's stress on the humanness of Jesus can again be a needed corrective.

Mark's Jesus is one who experienced the world much as we do, a village woodworker whose life was so ordinary that those who knew him best did not regard him as exceptional. Then, with the suddenness that is characteristic of Mark, all that changed when the Nazarene presented himself for John's baptism of repentance and found his life drastically uprooted by a call to serve God completely.

In fulfilling that mission Mark's Jesus found himself alienated from family and friends, opposed by the leaders of his religion and in serious danger. He knew grief, indignation, anger, frustration, betrayal and even frustrated love. Aware of his ultimate fate, he shrank from it and prayed to be spared, but accepted his fate in obedience to One he addressed as "Abba."

Mark's presentation of so human a Jesus demands that the reader accept a Jesus who underwent very human suffering and death, not somehow immunized from the agony by being divine. Above all Mark stresses that Jesus faced death with the same trust in God that is asked of us. The "Eloi, Eloi, lema sabachthani?" ("My God, my God, why have you forsaken me?") of Jesus shows that Jesus' trust in God was really challenged. Yet Jesus remained confident to the end: "[The LORD] did not hide his face from me, but heard when I cried to him." (Psalm 22:24)

Mark can achieve for us today what he hoped to accomplish for his own Christian community. He wanted to counterbalance a too ready acceptance of Jesus' divinity at the expense of his humanity. Mark may have felt that an overly divinized Jesus would seem remote from and insensitive to the challenges facing the Christians of his day. An unknown Christian who wrote around the same time as Mark put it this way: "For we do not have a high priest [Jesus] who is unable to sympathize with our weaknesses, but we have one who in every respect has been tested as we are, yet without sin." (Hebrews 4:15) Mark would have agreed wholeheartedly.

STUDY QUESTIONS

1. In affirming the divinity of Jesus what challenge faced the author of the first Gospel?
2. How does the first Gospel meet this challenge in its depiction of Jesus before his public life?
3. What are some of the limitations Jesus exhibited in his public life?
4. What emotions did Jesus display?
5. In what ways does Mark's Gospel stress Jesus' humanity during the Passion?
6. Why would Mark's readers have a particularly realistic vision of Jesus' death on the cross?
7. Who might have been the living link between Mark's community and Jesus' final hours?
8. In what ways does Mark's Jesus resemble the ideal Roman?

9. What were the reactions of the Gospels of Matthew and Luke to Mark's depiction of Jesus?
10. What is the reaction of the Gospel of John?
11. What further reaction do we find in the letters attributed to John?
12. What relevance does the depiction of Jesus have for us today?

Chapter Nine

THE WONDERWORKER

I. WONDROUS DEEDS IN MARK

Certainly the most striking characteristic about Mark's Jesus is his ability to do remarkable deeds. Of the four hundred and twenty-five verses that make up the first ten chapters of the first Gospel, two hundred are devoted to the wondrous exploits of Jesus. They begin with his "debut" in the synagogue of Capernaum when he exorcises an unclean spirit (1:23–26). They end on the outskirts of Jericho where Jesus restores the sight of Bartimaeus (10:46–52). In fact, one or more wondrous deeds occur in each of these first chapters.

The variety of the deeds is no less impressive. During Jesus' public life he is seen curing a fever (1:30–31), leprosy (1:40ff), paralysis (2:3ff), a withered hand (3:1ff), internal bleeding (5:25ff), a deaf mute (7:32ff), blindness (8:22ff; 10:46). On one occasion, it would appear that Jesus brought a child back to life (5:22ff). He also performed exorcisms, the driving out of evil spirits (1:23–27; 5:2; 7:26).

In addition to these individual incidents, Mark recounts that in Capernaum, the "whole city was gathered around the door [where Jesus was staying]. And he cured many who were sick with various diseases, and cast out many demons." (1:33–34) Wherever Jesus appeared, "all who had diseases pressed upon him to touch him." (3:10) When he was recognized, all the people "rushed about that whole region and began to bring the sick on mats to wherever they heard he was. And wherever Jesus went, into villages or cities or farms, they laid the sick in the marketplaces, and begged him that they might touch even the fringe of his cloak; and all who touched it were healed." (6:55–56) Jesus also calmed storms at sea (4:37–39; 6:41), walked on the sea (6:48) and on two occasions fed a large number of people on small amounts of food (6:33–44; 8:1–9). These wondrous acts of Jesus form an integral part of Mark's Gospel.

II. THE ATTITUDE OF MARK'S READERS

Yet, it is in our view of these wondrous deeds that we and the first readers of Mark differ greatly. We would call these actions of Jesus "miracles."[1] The *Oxford English Dictionary* defines a miracle as "a remarkable and welcome event that seems impossible to explain by means of known laws of nature and is therefore attributed to a supernatural agency." This is a relatively modern concept born of the conviction that there are immutable "laws of nature" that govern the universe. Any violation of these laws is taken by the believer to be the result of a direct intervention by God. The non-believer, naturally, would hesitate to come to such a conclusion. Rather, he would say that if such an exception did occur, it would actually be the result of some law of nature we do not yet fully understand.

Such a debate would be lost on Mark's community. They shared the outlook of the Hebrew Bible where there is no such notion of the laws of nature. As we find in McKenzie's *Dictionary of the Bible*, "The whole of nature is personalized, and there is no idea of natural causes acting according to constant laws and fixed principles." (p. 578a) Like the Jews, Christians attributed to God's will whatever occurred.

Like the pagans, Christians believed that demons or evil spirits could also cause some events but only if God allowed them to. We can see this reflected in the letter to the Ephesians, attributed to Paul, where we have: "For our struggle is not against enemies of blood and flesh, but...against the cosmic powers of this present darkness, against the spiritual forces of evil in the heavenly places." (6:12) The view of Mark's pagan contemporaries was not substantially different. Only their attribution would have been to the various gods.

Mark's readers would have been aware that wonders were supposed to have occurred in the Gentile world, especially in connection with the "rich and famous." Suetonius in *The Twelve Caesars* tells us: "When Octavius [Emperor Augustus' father] arrived late because of Atia's [his mother's] confinement, Publius Nigidius Figulus the astrologer, hearing at what hour the child had been delivered, cried out, 'The ruler of the world is now born.'" (p. 105) The historian also reports that as an infant, Augustus disappeared from his crib, only to reappear on a high tower with his face to the sun. While still a child he silenced the frogs in a pond. No frog ever croaked in that pond again. His predecessor, Julius Caesar, thinking it a sign of victory, spared a palm tree from being cut down. Subsequently, a new shoot from the tree, in but a few days, outgrew and overshadowed its source. Though very unlikely for them to do so, a flock of doves nested in the dominant shoot of the tree. When Augustus took power after the death of Julius Caesar, there were numerous remarkable signs. (*Op. cit.* pp. 106-107)

For us miracles are by definition rare and we tend to be skeptical about reports of their occurrence. Mark's Christians had no such bias. Moreover, they would certainly have expected Jesus' life to be accompanied by remarkable deeds, just as such exploits accompanied the lives of other impressive personages in public life. Yet, Mark is doing more than simply signaling that Jesus was an exceptionally powerful being. What must also be noted is the other role that Jesus' deeds of power play in the first Gospel.

III. SIGNS OF AUTHORITY

We get a clue to a reason for Mark's recounting Jesus' deeds of power from something that occurred not long before his Gospel was written. Suetonius writes that in 69 C.E. the following took place: "Vespasian, still rather bewildered in his new role of Emperor, felt a certain lack of authority and impressiveness; yet both these attributes were granted him. As he sat on the Tribunal, two laborers, one blind, the other lame, approached him together, begging to be healed. Apparently the god Serapis had promised them in a dream that if Vespasian would consent to spit in the blind man's eyes, and touch the lame man's leg with his heel, both would be made well.... the charm worked." (*Op. cit.* p. 284) As a result of the "deed of power" Vespasian gains in both "authority and impressiveness."

Similarly the Hebrew Bible is replete with examples of deeds of power that authenticate missions of those sent to Israel by God. When Moses fears that the people of Israel will not believe that he has been sent to them by God, we have the following: "The LORD said to

[Moses], 'What is that in your hand?' He said, 'A staff.' And he said, 'Throw it on the ground.' So he threw the staff on the ground, and it became a snake; and Moses drew back from it. Then the LORD said to Moses, 'Reach out your hand, and seize it by the tail'—so he reached out his hand and grasped it, and it became a staff in his hand—'so that they may believe that the LORD, the God of their ancestors, the God of Abraham, the God of Isaac, and the God of Jacob, has appeared to you.'" (Exodus 4:3–5) The first of the prophets, Elijah, is introduced by a series of deeds of power and his authority is recognized: "So the woman said to Elijah, 'Now I know that you are a man of God, and that the word of the LORD in your mouth is truth.'" (I Kings 17:24)

Similarly, Paul pointed to "signs and wonders" as authenticating his mission as an apostle: "The signs of a true apostle were performed among you with utmost patience, signs and wonders and mighty works." (II Corinthians 12:12) He boasts in the letter to the Romans: "By the power of signs and wonders, by the power of the Spirit of God, from Jerusalem and as far around as Illyricum I have fully proclaimed the good news of Christ." (15:19)

Mark reflects a similar view when he speaks of the mission of apostles to preach the Good News: "[Jesus] appointed twelve, whom he also named apostles, to be with him, and to be sent out to proclaim the message, and to have authority to cast out demons." (3:14–15) Later, Mark tells the reader, "They cast out many demons, and anointed with oil many who were sick and cured them." (6:13) Deeds of power, miracles if you will, authenticate the missions of those sent by God. The same would have been expected of Jesus.

IV. THE AUTHORITY OF JESUS

When Jesus first appears in the synagogue at Capernaum we are told that his hearers "were astounded at his teaching, for he taught them as one having authority." (1:22) That authority is immediately reinforced when Jesus is confronted by a man under the control of an unclean spirit. The spirit is driven out and the onlookers react: "What is this? A new teaching—with authority! He commands even the unclean spirits, and they obey him." (1:27) As with those mentioned above, Jesus' authority is enhanced by a deed of power.

Of course, as Mark points out, not everyone was necessarily impressed. The problem for some was that they had known Jesus during the years preceding his public life. When Jesus' fellow Nazareans are confronted by him in their synagogue, they ask, "Where did this man get all this? What is this wisdom that has been given to him? What deeds of power are being done by his hands!" (6:2) They were actually offended by his claims. Jesus' own family was apparently similarly unimpressed (3:21).

V. THE EXORCIST

One group of Jesus' deeds of power requires special consideration, his exorcisms. Mark's Christians, no less than the people of Jesus' time, believed in the existence of "the spiritual forces of evil in the heavenly places." (Ephesians 6:12) By driving out such forces, Jesus demonstrated his power over evil, something that would have been expected of the one who was to herald the coming of the parousia. Thus, we see Jesus performing a series of exorcisms, including his first deed of power (1:23–27), as well as the expelling of a "legion" of demons from the Gerasene man found wandering in the tombs (5:2), and an unclean spirit from the daughter of the Syrophoenician woman (7:26). In Capernaum, we are told, Jesus "cast out many demons." (1:34) Jesus also extended the power to exorcise to his disciples (3:15).

Nevertheless, the demonstration of power over evil is not an unambiguous sign. The demons themselves were regarded as having powers, powers they could turn against their own kind. Mark tells the reader that such a charge was leveled against Jesus: "And the scribes who came down from Jerusalem said, 'He has Beelzebul,[2] and by the ruler of the demons he casts out demons.'" (3:22) Mark shows the ridiculousness of the charge:

> [Jesus] called [his disciples] to him, and spoke to them in parables, "How can Satan[3] cast out Satan? If a kingdom is divided against itself, that kingdom cannot stand. And if a house is divided against itself, that house will not be able to stand. And if Satan has risen up against himself and is divided, he cannot stand, but his end has come. But no one can

enter a strong man's house and plunder his property without first tying up the strong man; then indeed the house can be plundered." (3:23–27)

VI. THE HEALER

It must also be observed that at the time of both Jesus and Mark there was no strict distinction between exorcising and healing. Actually it was assumed that all diseases were caused by demons or some sort of "unclean spirit." Vermes notes: "In the world of Jesus, the devil was believed to be at the basis of sickness as well as sin." (*Op. cit.* p. 61) This is reflected in the account of Jesus' cure of the epileptic boy: "Someone from the crowd answered [Jesus], 'Teacher, I brought you my son; he has a spirit that makes him unable to speak; and whenever it seizes him, it dashes him down; and he foams and grinds his teeth and becomes rigid; and I asked your disciples to cast it out, but they could not do so.'" (9:17–18) The child is cured when Jesus drives off the spirit. The joining of exorcism and healing is further stressed in the scene that follows: "[Jesus'] disciples asked him privately, 'Why could we not cast it out?' He said to them, 'This kind can come out only through prayer.'" (9:28–29)

The incident would be quite understandable to Mark's readers at a time when medicine was a mixture of primitive medical technique, religion and magic. Aescalapius, a god imported by the Romans from Greece, was thought to be particularly effective in the cures of illness, and a temple in his honor was erected on an island in the Tiber near the center of Rome. There the sick were brought for treatment, and there, as well, prayers and sacrifices were offered for their cure.[4] Similar shrines existed throughout the empire.

Mark's readers would have had no reason to question the tradition that Jesus performed these deeds of power. Actually, they would have expected them from one they believed to be the Son of God. At the same time, compared to the popular accounts of miraculous deeds accomplished by mythological and real figures, Mark is actually restrained. Again his is a task of delicate balance, weighing Jesus' humanity and his divinity, the particular challenge being not to let the latter overshadow the former.

VII. THE ROLE OF FAITH

A. *The Meaning of Faith*

Relating to Jesus' deeds of power, another theme runs through Mark. We see Jesus frequently demanding "faith" of those who are cured of their afflictions. The Greek *pisteuein* can be translated as both "to trust in" and "to hold as true." In the context of Mark, "trust" is the better meaning. At times, it appears that trusting in Jesus plays a role in being cured by Jesus.

Here again we may be seeing the influence of Paul. In one form or another, the word is found in the writings of the apostle over two hundred times, almost fifty of which are in his letter to Rome. He compliments that Christian community saying, "I thank my God through Jesus Christ for all of you, because your faith is proclaimed throughout the world." (1:8) The apostle's crucial point is that "a person is justified by faith apart from works prescribed by the law." (3:28) In the first Gospel, Jesus begins his public mission demanding "faith" of his followers: "The time is fulfilled, and the kingdom of God has come near; repent, and [trust] in the good news." (1:15) It is in the accounts of Jesus' deeds of power that Mark shows the role of that faith most clearly.

B. *Faith and the Deeds of Power*

In a particularly vivid scene, we are told, "Some people came, bringing to [Jesus] a paralyzed man, carried by four of them. And when they could not bring him to Jesus because of the crowd, they removed the roof above him; and after having dug through it, they let down the mat on which the paralytic lay. When Jesus saw their faith, he said to the paralytic, 'Son, your sins are forgiven.'" (2:3–5) It is not the faith of the paralytic himself that results in his cure, it is the trust displayed by his friends.

We have also the account of "a woman who had been suffering from hemorrhages for twelve years. She had endured much under many physicians, and had spent all that she had; and she was no better, but rather grew worse." (5:25–26) Obviously, she had misplaced her trust, possibly a Marcan jab at the medical practitioners of his day. Now, trustingly, the woman approaches Jesus: "If I but touch his clothes, I will be made well." (5:28) She is cured and Jesus tells her, "Daughter, your faith has made you well; go in peace, and be healed of your disease." (5:34) Mark may have intended to contrast the ineffective faith placed in physicians with the efficacious trust in Jesus.

We see the same dynamic between faith and Jesus' deeds of power in the following: "Then one of the leaders of the synagogue named Jairus came and, when he saw him, fell at his feet and begged him repeatedly, 'My little daughter is at the point of death. Come and lay your hands on her, so that she may be made well, and live.'" (5:22–23) However, before they get to Jairus' home, "some people came from the leader's house to say, 'Your daughter is dead. Why trouble the teacher any further?' (5:36) When Jesus hears this he tells the grieving father, "Do not fear, only believe." (5:37) The man's faith is rewarded: "[Jesus] took her by the hand and said to her, 'Talitha cum,' which means, 'Little girl, get up!' And immediately the girl got up and began to walk about (she was twelve years of age). At this they were overcome with amazement." (5:41–42) In a nice touch, Jesus tells her parents to get her something to eat.

We have already mentioned the cure of the epileptic child. There the father pleads with Jesus, "[The evil spirit] has often cast him into the fire and into the water, to destroy him; but if you are able to do anything, have pity on us and help us." (9:22) To this Jesus replies, "If you are able!—All things can be done for the one who believes." (9:23) It is not what Jesus can do that is essential, it is faith. "Immediately the father of the child cried out, 'I believe; help my unbelief!'" (9:24) Yet, limited though the father's trust might have been, Jesus still cures his son. Mark appears to offer hope to the believer, however circumscribed is that believer's faith.

It seems also to work both ways; trusting in Jesus empowers him to exorcise or cure; on the other hand, lack of trust limits that power. Mark shows us this when Jesus returns to his home town. As we saw earlier, his fellow Nazarenes are unable to accept him as anyone out of the ordinary. In fact "they took offense at him." (6:3) As a result Mark tells us, "[Jesus] could do no deed of power there, except that he laid his hands on a few sick people and cured them. And he was amazed at their unbelief." (6:5–6)

C. The Testimony to Faith

When we come to the final phase of Jesus' life, Mark gives the reader testimony to the power of faith in the words of Jesus: "Have faith in God. Truly I tell you, if you say to this mountain, 'Be taken up and thrown into the sea,' and if you do not doubt in your heart, but believe that what you say will come to pass, it will be done for you. So I tell you, whatever you ask for in prayer, believe that you have received it, and it will be yours." (11:22–24)

Mark's readers lived in a world where others made claims to "deeds of power," others claimed to be able to exorcise evil spirits and still others offered cures for diseases. Since these claims were wrapped in pagan practices, the Christians were denied their supposed benefits. Placing one's trust in Jesus was a challenge that had to be faced again and again. At times, the temptation to compromise must have been intense. The cry of the epileptic boy's father must have been the plea of many a Christian in Mark's time: "I believe; help my unbelief!" (9:24)

STUDY QUESTIONS

1. Are wondrous deeds characteristic of Jesus' public life?
2. In what ways does the modern view of a miracle differ from the view of Mark's Christians?
3. What is the function of the wondrous deed in Mark's Gospel?
4. Why are exorcisms of special importance in Mark's depiction of Jesus?
5. Why is it not easy to distinguish between exorcism and healing in Mark's Gospel?
6. What is the significance of Jesus' stress on faith's role in his cures?

Chapter Ten

THE TEACHER AND HIS TEACHINGS

I. THE TEACHER

In the first Gospel, Jesus is referred to as "teacher" thirteen times. The title is used by his disciples (4:38; 9:38; 10:35; 13:1), by his enemies (12:14,19), by Jesus himself (14:14) and by others (5:35; 9:17; 10:17,20,51; 12:32). Twice, Peter calls Jesus by the Hebrew term for "teacher," "rabbi." (9:5; 11:21) Similarly, Judas, at the moment of betrayal, uses "rabbi" to address Jesus (14:44). From the very beginning of his public life Jesus is shown teaching: "They went to Capernaum; and when the sabbath came, [Jesus] entered the synagogue and taught. They were astounded at his teaching, for he taught them as one having authority, and not as the scribes." (1:21–22)

Jesus taught by the seashore (4:1; 6:34), in the villages of Galilee (6:6) and in their synagogues (1:21; 1:39), including Nazareth's (6:2). Finally, as his career comes to a close, Jesus' holds forth in the great temple of Jerusalem (11:17; 12:14ff; 12:35). Many of Jesus' teachings were directed to the crowds that followed him, his enemies included, but some were meant for the special instruction of Jesus' own disciples (4:34; 7:17; 9:31; 10:10; 13:1ff).

A familiar sight to Mark's community would have been the itinerant philosopher, surrounded by his followers, lecturing in one of Rome's *basilicae* or *fora* to whatever crowd might gather. There were also those with the role of teacher in the Christian local and house churches as Vincent Branick observes: "Teachers (*didaskaloi*) probably functioned in the church much like those Jews who bore the same name—giving instructions, delivering ethical exhortations, receiving and preserving, transmitting the traditions, interpreting scripture." (*Op. cit.* p. 82) Mark's community would have seen Jesus as fulfilling a similar role.

Yet in only two places does Mark record at any length the content of Jesus' teachings (4:21–25; 9:41–50). For instance, there is nothing in the first Gospel to match Matthew's Sermon on the Mount (5:1–7:29). A possible explanation would be Mark's view that the parousia was soon to come. As the time remaining was short a detailed instruction was not needed; only the essentials were required. As a result, Jesus' teaching on any subject tends to be brief and distributed throughout the Gospel narrative. The exceptions, however, are the parables.[1]

II. THE PARABLES

A. *Characteristic of Jesus' Teaching*

Mark does preserve what apparently was a feature of Jesus' style in teaching. "With many such parables he spoke the word to them, as they were able to hear it; he did not speak to them except in parables." (4:33–34) In his *The Parables of the Kingdom*, C.H. Dodd notes: "The parables are perhaps the most characteristic element in the teaching of Jesus Christ as recorded in the Gospels. They have upon them, taken as a whole, the stamp of a highly individual mind, in spite of the re-handling they have inevitably suffered in the course of transmission. Their appeal to the imagination fixed them in the memory, and gave them a secure place in the tradition. Certainly there is no part of the Gospel record, which has for the reader a clearer ring of authenticity." (p. 13)

Any teacher or preacher knows how forceful a story can be in making a point. Æsop told the story of a fox struggling to reach the grapes only to walk away muttering that they were probably sour anyway. Simply stating that we tend to undervalue what we cannot have would convey the same message but nowhere near as memorably. Jesus of Nazareth, like the rabbis of his day, was aware of the effectiveness of a story. Though Mark has fewer parables than either Matthew or Luke, they play an important role in the first Gospel.

B. *Interpretation*

1. THE ROLE OF ALLEGORY

Before turning to the parables themselves an important point must be noted. Joachim Jeremias in his *The Parables of Jesus* observes:

As they have come down to us, the parables of Jesus have a double historical setting. (1) The original historical setting of the parables, as of all his utterances, is some specific situation in the pattern of the activity of Jesus. Many of the parables are so vividly told that it is natural to assume that they arise out of some actual occurrence. (2) But subsequently, before they assumed a written form, they "lived" in the primitive Church, of whose proclamations, preaching, and teaching, the words of Jesus were content, in its missionary activities, in its assemblies, or in its catechetical instruction.... it is important to bear in mind the difference between the situation of Jesus and that of the primitive Church. (p. 23)

One such "primitive church" was Mark's. As we have stressed, these Christians lived their faith in an urban setting quite different from the rural environment in which Jesus himself taught. In making the transition setting to the other, the parable in Mark fulfills a different purpose from its original one.

Jesus would have used the parable to make his point with greater clarity, but in Mark Jesus is shown to use the story to obscure his message. "When [Jesus] was alone, those who were around him along with the twelve asked him about the parables. And he said to them, 'To you has been given the secret of the kingdom of God, but for those outside, everything comes in parables, in order that "they may indeed look, but not perceive, and may indeed listen, but not understand, so that they may not turn again and be forgiven." ' " (4:10–12) The quote is from Isaiah (6:9–10) and the prophet's point is ironic; the last thing his hearers want to do is to understand. Thus, the purpose of the parable is to conceal Jesus' message.

For Mark, then, the parable is a kind of code in which each element in the story has a hidden significance. This is to understand the parable as an allegory, a mode of literary interpretation common in Mark's time. The Jewish scholar Philo (c. 20 B.C.E.–c. 41 C.E.) used the method to make the Jewish traditions meaningful to the Greek culture. Mark appears to have done the same to make the parables of Jesus comprehensible to his own readers. Examining one of the parables will help us to see this.

2. THE WICKED TENANTS

Scripture scholars agree that some of the words and deeds of Jesus may have been preserved in works that were never accepted by the church as sacred Scripture. One such work is *The Gospel of Thomas.*[2] It contains a version of the parable of the wicked tenants which is earlier than the one found in Mark:

> A person owned a vineyard and rented it to some farmers, so they might work it and he might collect its produce from them. He sent his servant so that the farmers might give the servant the produce of the vineyard. They seized, beat and almost killed his servant, and the servant returned and told his master. His master said, "Perhaps he did not know them." He sent another servant, and the farmers beat that one as well. The master sent his son and said, "Perhaps they will show my son some respect." Since the farmers knew that he was the heir to the vineyard, they seized him and killed him. Whoever has ears should hear. (p. 53 #65)

Given the unsettled and even rebellious situation in Galilee at his time, Jesus may have been recalling an actual event. The tenant farmers of the parable may have had the sympathies of Jesus' hearers, many of whom must have suffered the oppression of absentee landlords. The violence aside, the tenants could have been seen as seizing what was rightfully theirs. Speaking of the early form of the parable, Jeremias notes, "Like so many other parables of Jesus it vindicates the offer of the gospel to the poor." (*Op. cit.* p. 76) Unfortunately, lacking the context of the parable at its origin we cannot be sure of the point Jesus was making.

Mark himself may have had no more knowledge than we of the parable's original meaning. His version is an adaptation of the story to new circumstances:

> A man planted a vineyard, put a fence around it, dug a pit for the wine press, and built a watchtower; then he leased it to tenants and went to another country. When the season came, he sent a slave to the tenants to collect from them his share of the produce of the vineyard. But they seized him, and beat him, and sent him away empty-handed. And again he sent another slave to them; this one they beat over the head and

insulted. Then he sent another, and that one they killed. And so it was with many others; some they beat, and others they killed. He had still one other, a beloved son. Finally he sent him to them, saying, "They will respect my son." But those tenants said to one another, "This is the heir; come, let us kill him, and the inheritance will be ours." So they seized him, killed him, and threw him out of the vineyard. What then will the owner of the vineyard do? He will come and destroy the tenants and give the vineyard to others. (12:1–10)

Note the changes that Mark makes in the earlier version: he adds a description of the construction of the vineyard; he expands the number of slaves sent and their fates; the son becomes "a beloved son"; after being killed he is thrown out of the vineyard; finally the punishment of his murderers is described—they are destroyed and replaced. As Jeremias points out, "The whole parable is evidently pure allegory." (*Op. cit.* p. 70)

The key to understanding Mark's rendering of the parable lies in the depiction of the vineyard's fashioning. Mark has recalled the words of Isaiah:

Let me sing for my beloved my love-song concerning his vineyard: My beloved had a vineyard on a very fertile hill. He dug it and cleared it of stones, and planted it with choice vines; he built a watchtower in the midst of it, and hewed out a wine vat in it; he expected it to yield grapes, but it yielded wild grapes.... And now I will tell you what I will do to my vineyard. I will remove its hedge, and it shall be devoured; I will break down its wall, and it shall be trampled down.... For the vineyard of the LORD of hosts is the house of Israel. (5:1–2,5,7)

From the perspective of an allegory the vineyard represents God's chosen people, once loved but now rejected and replaced by those who follow Jesus. The destruction of the vineyard would have been seen as fulfilled in the fate of Jerusalem. Other elements are similarly allegorized; the temple leadership are the wicked tenants; the prophets sent to Israel are the slaves; Jesus is the "beloved son"—all changes meaningful to Mark's readers.

III. THE PARABLES OF THE KINGDOM[3]

A. *The Kingdom in the Jewish Tradition*

The "kingdom of God" lies at the core of the Gospel message as we find it in Mark. "Now after John [the Baptist] was arrested, Jesus came to Galilee, proclaiming the good news of God, and saying, 'The time is fulfilled, and the kingdom of God has come near; repent, and believe in the good news.'" (1:14–15) Its coming is to characterize the parousia. As part of the Jewish tradition, it was an expression familiar to Jesus' hearers.

The prospect of a future divine kingdom is found in the Hebrew Bible: "The LORD has established his throne in the heavens, and his kingdom rules over all." (Psalm 103:19) "All your works shall give thanks to you, O LORD, and all your faithful shall bless you. They shall speak of the glory of your kingdom, and tell of your power, to make known to all people your mighty deeds, and the glorious splendor of your kingdom. Your kingdom is an everlasting kingdom, and your dominion endures throughout all generations." (Psalm 145:10–13)

One reads in the book of Daniel: "The signs and wonders that the Most High God has worked for me I am pleased to recount. How great are his signs, how mighty his wonders! His kingdom is an everlasting kingdom, and his sovereignty is from generation to generation." (4:2–3) In speaking of the "one like a human being" the prophet writes: "To him was given dominion and glory and kingship, that all peoples, nations, and languages should serve him. His dominion is an everlasting dominion that shall not pass away, and his kingship is one that shall never be destroyed." (7:14) The link between "the son of man" and the coming of the kingdom of God is central to Mark.

As McKenzie points out: "The idea of kingdom is more frequent in Jewish apocalyptic literature. The kingdom here is not only the catastrophic display of power and judgment but also the establishment of the reign of God.... These allusions show that Jesus could employ the term with no introductory explanation; but the [New Testament] idea of the kingdom of God is not dependent on apocalyptic literature except in some details of imagery." (*Op. cit.* pp.

479–481) Mark undoubtedly received the tradition that Jesus used "the kingdom of God" as a way of expressing his expectations for the future.

B. The Kingdom in Paul

In the authentic letters of the apostle the "kingdom of God" appears as a reward for those who are virtuous and something lost to those who are not (see I Thessalonians 2:12; Galatians 5:21; I Corinthians 6:9–10; Romans 14:17). On only one occasion in Paul is the "kingdom" connected with the parousia: "Then comes the end, when he hands over the kingdom to God the Father, after he has destroyed every ruler and every authority and power." (I Corinthians 15:24) In view of this, Joseph Fitzmyer asserts that the " 'kingdom of God' is hardly an operative element in Pauline teaching." (*NJBC*, p. 1413b) The apostle's uses of the phrase Fitzmyer calls "elements of pre-Pauline catechetical instruction, which he inherited and made use of." (*Ibid.*) The same tradition came as well to the first evangelist.

C. The Kingdom of God in Mark

As with Paul, Mark's "kingdom of God" is the reward for a virtuous life. "Let the little children come to me; do not stop them; for it is to such as these that the kingdom of God belongs. Truly I tell you, whoever does not receive the kingdom of God as a little child will never enter it." (10:14–15; see also 9:47; 10:23–25; 12:34). The coming of the "kingdom" also inaugurates the parousia. Jesus warns his followers, "Truly I tell you, there are some standing here who will not taste death until they see that the kingdom of God has come with power." (9:1; see also 14:25; 15:43) Three of the six parables found in Mark are concerned with the "kingdom of God."

D. The Parable of The Sower

1. THE ORIGINAL VERSION

It would have been to his readers that Mark addressed the words of Jesus, "To you has been given the secret of the kingdom of God, but for those outside, everything comes in parables." (4:11) The parable of immediate concern was that of "The Sower":

Listen! A sower went out to sow. And as he sowed, some seed fell on the path, and the birds came and ate it up. Other seed fell on rocky ground, where it did not have much soil, and it sprang up quickly, since it had no depth of soil. And when the sun rose, it was scorched; and since it had no root, it withered away. Other seed fell among thorns, and the thorns grew up and choked it, and it yielded no grain. Other seed fell into good soil and brought forth grain, growing up and increasing and yielding thirty and sixty and a hundredfold. (4:1–8)

Mark's version of the parable is close to the one found in *The Gospel of Thomas*:

Look, the sower went out, took a handful (of seeds), and scattered (them). Some fell on the road, and the birds came and pecked them up. Others fell on rock, and they did not take root in the soil and did not produce heads of grain. Others fell on thorns, and they choked the seeds and worms devoured them. And others fell on good soil, and it brought forth a good crop: it yielded sixty per measure, and one hundred and twenty per measure. (p. 25 #9)

The parable has the ring of authenticity since it depicts planting as it would have been carried out in Jesus' time. It is not all that different from the method still employed in parts of the middle east today. In a dry climate too much moisture would be lost in plowing the field and then sowing the seed. Thus the seed is spread on the dry ground and then the soil is turned over.

Now, during the off-season villagers tramping across the field leave paths on which the seed falls and much of it is lost to the birds. The characteristic rocky ground and thorny bushes take their toll. Yet, in spite of all the losses, there is a harvest and, at times, an abundant one. In telling the parable Jesus sought to reassure his hearers. To the farmers and villagers of Galilee the power of Rome might seem overwhelming, leaving little hope for the future. Nevertheless, Jesus is saying, just as the bountiful harvest is unexpected, so will be the coming of the kingdom of God at the parousia.

2. MARCAN INTERPRETATION

Mark and his readers, of course, were well aware that the parousia did not immediately follow the public life of Jesus. In the light of this,

Mark did not change the parable. Rather, the first evangelist added an allegorical interpretation of the story:

> The sower sows the word. These are the ones on the path where the word is sown: when they hear, Satan immediately comes and takes away the word that is sown in them. And these are the ones sown on rocky ground: when they hear the word, they immediately receive it with joy. But they have no root, and endure only for a while; then, when trouble or persecution arises on account of the word, immediately they fall away. And others are those sown among the thorns: these are the ones who hear the word, but the cares of the world, and the lure of wealth, and the desire for other things come in and choke the word, and it yields nothing. And these are the ones sown on the good soil: they hear the word and accept it and bear fruit, thirty and sixty and a hundredfold. (4:14–20)

The parable now reflects, not the experiences of the Galileans in Jesus' time, but rather the experiences of Mark's Christian community. They have seen that the preaching of the word, the Good News, has no effect at all on some hearers. The evil in the world quickly obliterates it. Others hear the Good News and, for a time at least, become enthusiastic disciples. Soon, in the face of the difficulties arising because of their new religion, they fall away. Other hearers remain disciples all right but are so caught up in daily affairs or so corrupted by the world around them that they make no contribution to the life of their church.

We have pointed out the many challenges facing these early Christians, surrounded as they were by a sea of paganism which was backed by great power and wealth. It is possible that, in the end, there would be only a relatively few followers of Jesus who would remain faithful. Nevertheless, with the coming of the parousia, these few would "bear fruit, thirty and sixty and a hundredfold." (4:20) By seeing the parable as an allegory Mark offers his readers the same encouragement that Jesus himself offered his hearers. The forces of evil may appear overwhelming but there will be an abundant harvest when the kingdom of God appears.

E. The Patient Farmer and the Mustard Seed

Mark includes two other parables with the rural flavor of "The Sower." They are not interpreted as allegories, but in the light of what we have just seen, we can surmise how they would have been understood by the reader. "The Patient Farmer" makes a point very similar to "The Sower," which may be why the other evangelists do not include it:

> The kingdom of God is as if someone would scatter seed on the ground, and would sleep and rise night and day, and the seed would sprout and grow, he does not know how. The earth produces of itself, first the stalk, then the head, then the full grain in the head. But when the grain is ripe, at once he goes in with his sickle, because the harvest has come. (4:26–29)

Mark again reassures his readers by pointing out that the harvest is after all not the result of the farmers' efforts but is the work of nature. Similarly, the victory over evil that will come with the parousia is not the achievement of the Christians, it is the triumph of God.

The brief parable of "The Mustard Seed" is also meant to encourage Mark's readers:

> With what can we compare the kingdom of God, or what parable will we use for it? It is like a mustard seed, which, when sown upon the ground, is the smallest of all the seeds on earth; yet when it is sown it grows up and becomes the greatest of all shrubs, and puts forth large branches, so that the birds of the air can make nests in its shade. (4:30–33; see also *The Gospel of Thomas*, p. 33 #20)

We have already observed that Mark's community did not number more than a few dozen. There were probably other Christian communities in Rome, but even if they were included the total would have been minuscule relative to three quarters of a million inhabitants of the capital city. Such an insignificant group held out little hope for the glorious future Jesus promised. So, Mark is saying, neither does the tiny mustard seed show evidence of the great plant it will become. The kingdom of God, when it arrives, will transcend the meager present evidence of what is to come.

IV. ROME AND THE KINGDOM OF GOD

We have noted that Mark was sensitive to how his writings might be understood by his fellow Romans, particularly government officials.

Speaking of a coming "kingdom" would not seem politic. Movements for independence were seen as a threat and the recent uprising in Palestine made the matter even more touchy. Christians needed to be especially cautious as their founder, Jesus of Nazareth, had been executed as an insurrectionist, his imputed claim being attached to the cross itself, "The King of the Jews." (15:26)

It is likely that Mark, to counteract the charge, is careful to present the "kingdom of God" as something in the future and otherworldly. Moreover, the kingdom is not to be established by human effort, certainly not by rebellion. You might say that Mark "depoliticized" the kingdom of God as foretold by Jesus. The problem, however, did not go away apparently. A generation later, when the final Gospel is written, its author must again refute the charge, this time directly. In John's Gospel when Pilate asks Jesus if he is the King of the Jews, the reply is, "My kingdom is not from this world. If my kingdom were from this world, my followers would be fighting to keep me from being handed over to the Jews. But as it is, my kingdom is not from here." (8:36)

STUDY QUESTIONS

1. Though the Gospel of Mark calls Jesus a teacher, there are few examples of what he taught. Why is this?
2. What is a "parable"?
3. What characterizes an allegorical interpretation of a parable?
4. How is this demonstrated in Mark's version of "The Wicked Tenants"?
5. What is the "Kingdom of God" in the Jewish traditions? In Paul? In Mark's Gospel?
6. In interpreting the "Parable of the Sower" how does the Gospel of Mark reflect a change in perspective from the parable's original setting?
7. How would Mark's Christians have understood the parables of "The Patient Farmer" and "The Mustard Seed"?
8. Why was the phrase the "Kingdom of God" troublesome for Mark's community?

Chapter Eleven

THE HOLY WEEK
PART ONE: SUNDAY TO TUESDAY

I. INTRODUCTION

A. *Change in Style*

The final chapters of Mark's Gospel bring striking changes in the author's style and presentation. For instance, up to now, the passage of time has been vague, so vague that there is no way of determining just how long Jesus' public life lasted. Similarly, the sites of many events are uncertain. Often we are not quite sure just where Jesus is. In contrast, when Mark recounts the closing days of Jesus' life, the place, the day, even the hour, are carefully noted. Moreover, the pace of the narration increases as we approach the climax, Jesus' death on the cross.

Such a shift in style gives a very dramatic tone to the closing scenes of the Gospel. We may have a clue here as to the form in which this part of the Gospel was first presented. Drama played an important role in the Hellenistic culture. Rome was particularly fascinated with the theater. "The smallest theater in Imperial Rome was still twice the size of the largest modern American theatre; and these dimensions would bear witness—if nothing else did—to the fact that the Roman's love of the theatre, though less consuming than his passion for the races, was still manifest." (Carcopino, *op. cit.* p. 222) Equally popular was the dramatic reading. It was the custom for an author to rent a space and invite friends and acquaintances to hear his new work.

It is thought possible that as part of an annual remembrance an account of the events surrounding Jesus' death and resurrection was recited in the Christian communities. In Mark we have a version of such a tradition, a version Mark edited to reflect the themes we have already mentioned. In view of his Roman audience, he may also have heightened the dramatic character of his presentation.[1]

There are two other changes in Mark's presentation of Jesus' final days. The first is in the role of the Pharisees. They were Jesus' chief opponents during the Galilean ministry; now they virtually disappear, being seen only once (12:13). In their place the high priest and his associates become the main antagonists of Jesus. Transferring Jesus' opposition from the Pharisees to Jerusalem's Jewish leadership has an advantage for Mark. Jesus' enemies now become the same as those who opposed the Romans in the Jewish war.

The other change is that Jesus does no deeds of power during these final days.[2] We have already noted that Mark places an emphasis on Jesus' humanity to counteract any tendency to see Jesus as a god in disguise. Certainly, nowhere in the first Gospel is Jesus more human than at the close of his life. His powerlessness in the face of his enemies gives further evidence of Jesus' humanity.

It should be noted that Mark's successors apparently felt he had overstated the point. Both Matthew and Luke seek to account for Jesus' failure to use his power to save himself. In Matthew Jesus says, "Do you think that I cannot appeal to my Father, and he will at once send me more than twelve legions of angels? But how then would the scriptures be fulfilled, which say it must happen in this way?" (26:53–54) In Luke Jesus restores the severed ear of the high priest's slave and then acknowledges, "But this is your hour, and the power of darkness!" (22:51,53) Finally, in John, Jesus has only to speak and the arresting party is thrown to the ground. When Peter seeks to defend Jesus, his answer is, "Put your sword back into its sheath. Am I not to drink the cup that the Father has given me?" (18:6,11) Each affirms that Jesus had the power to save himself, but chose not to use it.

B. The Final Days

Mark's account of the closing events in Jesus' life is arranged over a seven-day period.[3] It was mentioned earlier that prior to Mark the traditions surrounding these events were in oral form. The sequence of events we have probably came from a mnemonic used to aid the memory in transmitting the narrative. It is also possible that the arrangement reflected a week-long cycle of worship services during which the Christians celebrated the memory of the salvific events.

Another factor may also be reflected in Mark's sequence of events. It would not have been lost on the Christians in Rome that the resurrection of Jesus took place on the day of the week their pagan neighbors honored the sun, the ruling heavenly body. Placing the triumph of Jesus over death on the "day of the sun" may have been a way of hinting at Jesus' superiority over the gods of Rome. It would not be the last time that Christians would replace a pagan celebration with one of their own.[4]

Finally, as Mark's account of Jesus' Galilean ministry comes to a close and Jesus sets out for Jerusalem (10:32), we should recall what that city must have meant to the evangelist's readers. At the time of the first Gospel's writing, Jerusalem was virtually an abandoned ruin. Members of Mark's community may have known soldiers who witnessed Jerusalem's destruction. Christians who had once lived there may have migrated to the empire's capital, bringing their memories of Jerusalem's former glory. We have already noted that Christians living in Rome would have witnessed the treasures of the great temple paraded through the streets as part of Titus' triumph. Most importantly, Mark's Christians saw the destruction of the city and its temple as the sign announcing the imminent parousia. Jesus' entry into the holy city for the first time was most meaningful.

II. THE DAY OF THE SUN[5]

It is from Jericho that Jesus begins his journey up to Jerusalem. It is not without significance that it was there that Joshua fought a crucial battle when Israel entered the "promised land." (Joshua 6:20) At this point Mark recounts the following:

> As [Jesus] and his disciples and a large crowd were leaving Jericho, Bartimaeus son of Timaeus, a blind beggar, was sitting by the roadside. When he heard that it was Jesus of Nazareth, he began to shout out and say, "Jesus, Son of David, have mercy on me!" Many sternly ordered him to be quiet, but he cried out even more loudly, "Son of David, have mercy on me!" Jesus stood still and said, "Call him here." And they called the blind man, saying to him, "Take heart; get up, he is call-

ing you." So throwing off his cloak, he sprang up and came to Jesus. Then Jesus said to him, "What do you want me to do for you?" The blind man said to him, "My teacher, let me see again." Jesus said to him, "Go; your faith has made you well." Immediately he regained his sight and followed him on the way. (10:46-52)

As we have seen with earlier cures, because of his trust in the power of Jesus Bartimaeus regains his sight. Here, however, the one cured becomes a follower of Jesus which was not the case previously. Interestingly, what the blind man "sees" is that Jesus is the "son of David." He is the only one to apply that title to Jesus. Mark's readers would have been aware that Jerusalem is frequently called the "city of David" in the Hebrew Bible. Mark is carefully setting the scene.

When they were approaching Jerusalem, at Bethphage and Bethany, near the Mount of Olives, he sent two of his disciples and said to them, "Go into the village ahead of you, and immediately as you enter it, you will find tied there a colt that has never been ridden; untie it and bring it." ... Then they brought the colt to Jesus and threw their cloaks on it; and he sat on it. Many people spread their cloaks on the road, and others spread leafy branches that they had cut in the fields. Then those who went ahead and those who followed were shouting, "Hosanna! Blessed is the one who comes in the name of the Lord! Blessed is the coming kingdom of our ancestor David! Hosanna in the highest heaven!" (11:1-2,7-10)

Jesus' point of departure for his entry into Jerusalem, the Mount of Olives, will appear twice more in Mark's account of Jesus' final days. From there Jesus will view the city as he tells his disciples of his apocalyptic vision (13:3ff). After Jesus' final meal with his apostles, it will be on the same spot that Jesus predicts their desertion of him (14:27). Both latter instances would recall for the reader the prophecy of Zechariah where it is foretold that God will make an apocalyptic appearance on the final day standing on the Mount of Olives (14:4).

Mark's picture of Jesus arriving in Jerusalem is that of a triumphant procession. Yet, quite subtly, he undercuts the vision by his reference to a line from Zechariah: "Rejoice greatly, O daughter Zion! Shout aloud, O daughter Jerusalem! Lo, your king comes to you; triumphant and victorious is he, humble and riding on a donkey, on a colt, the foal of a donkey." (9:9) It is not as a victorious emperor that Jesus enters the city of David but unassumingly, without pomp and glory.

The cry of the crowd reflects one of the Psalms: "Save us,[6] we beseech you, O LORD! O LORD, we beseech you, give us success! Blessed is the one who comes in the name of the LORD." (118:25–26) The verse that follows may be implied: "The LORD is God, and he has given us light. Bind the festal procession with branches, up to the horns of the altar." (v. 27) And it is to the temple that Jesus goes: "Then he entered Jerusalem and went into the temple...." (11:11a) It is not as the conquering hero but as the religious pilgrim that Jesus comes into the holy city. It comes almost as an anticlimax that the reader is told, "when [Jesus] had looked around at everything, as it was already late, he went out to Bethany with the twelve." (11:11b)

III. THE DAY OF THE MOON

A. *The Cleansing of the Temple*

Mark's account of the second day in the holy week begins with a puzzling passage. On leaving Bethany, Jesus is hungry: "Seeing in the distance a fig tree in leaf, he went to see whether perhaps he would find anything on it. When he came to it, he found nothing but leaves, for it was not the season for figs. He said to it, 'May no one ever eat fruit from you again.' And his disciples heard it." (11:12–14) Why would Jesus seemingly punish the tree for being barren when it would not normally have any fruit? It is a question that Mark wants to place before the reader as his narrative continues.

Now Mark has Jesus return to the temple precincts: "Then they came to Jerusalem. And he entered the temple and began to drive out those who were selling and those who were buying in the temple, and he overturned the tables of the money changers and the seats of those who sold doves; and he would not allow anyone to carry anything through the temple." (11:15–16) Without the buying and selling and the money changing that made that commerce possible, the sacrificial rituals of the temple were at an end, a foreshadowing of what had occurred with the end of the Jewish war.

To justify his actions, Jesus says: "Is it not written, 'My house shall be called a house of prayer for all the nations'? But you have made it a den of robbers." (11:17) Here Isaiah's "My house shall be called a house of prayer for all peoples" (56:7) and Jeremiah's "Has this house ... become a den of robbers in your sight?" (7:11) have been combined. Jesus' accusation could be seen as Mark's explanation for the destruction of the temple in 70 C.E. Titus and his legions were carrying out the judgment of God, a judgment Jesus himself had first handed down.

B. The Opposition to Jesus

The import of Jesus' remarks are not lost on those Mark sees as Jesus' principal enemies: "When the chief priests and the scribes heard it, they kept looking for a way to kill him; for they were afraid of him, because the whole crowd was spellbound by his teaching." (11:18) Again, we point out that Mark's readers would see the opposition to Jesus as coming from those who also precipitated the disastrous revolt against Rome and brought about the very result Jesus' cleansing of the temple symbolized. Josephus writes that "the people [of Jerusalem] became so cowed and abject, and the terrorists so rabid, that they actually got control of the appointment of high priests." (*Op. cit.* p. 245) Though here the historian is overstating the situation, it was probably popularly held that the temple priesthood played a role in bringing about the disaster of 70 C.E. The day ending, Jesus and his followers leave the city for the night. (11:19)

IV. THE DAY OF MARS

A. The Challengers

1. THE CHIEF PRIESTS

When the account of day three opens, Mark returns to the cursed fig tree: "In the morning as they passed by, they saw the fig tree withered away to its roots. Then Peter remembered and said to him, 'Rabbi, look! The fig tree that you cursed has withered.'" (11:20–21) We have a parable "in action" which frames the symbolic destruction of the temple, now barren in the full sense, lying in ruins as it did in Mark's time. This reminder of Jerusalem's devastation serves the first evangelist as prologue to the challengers Jesus is about to face and defeat. Seeing the conflicts that now follow, one wonders if their occurrence on the day dedicated to the god of war is entirely coincidental. The first to confront Jesus are his principal enemies: "As he was walking in the temple, the chief priests, the scribes, and the elders came to him and said, 'By what authority are you doing these things? Who gave you this authority to do them?'" (11:27–28) Jesus' authority had been established by his deeds of power. Moreover, the Jerusalem authorities had already challenged Jesus on this point. "The scribes who came down from Jerusalem said, 'He has Beelzebul, and by the ruler of the demons he casts out demons.'" (3:22) Jesus showed the speciousness of that objection. Now, he takes another tack.

Jesus throws his challengers into confusion with a simple trap: "I will ask you one question; answer me, and I will tell you by what authority I do these things. Did the baptism of John come from heaven, or was it of human origin? Answer me." (11:29–30) His enemies are now caught on the horns of a dilemma. If they accept the heavenly origin of John's baptism, then Jesus can ask "Why then did you not believe him?" (11:31) On the other hand, if they opt for the ritual being of human origin, then they fear the crowd will turn on them, "for all regarded John as truly a prophet." (11:32) The reply of Jesus' opponents, "We do not know," exposes their insincerity and enables Jesus to say, "Neither will I tell you by what authority I am doing these things." (11:33)

It is here that Mark has placed Jesus' parable of "The Wicked Tenants" (12:1–9) which we saw in the previous chapter. Its targets stand before Jesus and the readers know their fate. As Jesus predicted, "[The owner] will come and destroy the tenants and give the vineyard to others." (12:9) Mark's Christians saw themselves as those who had now received God's favor. Again, Mark makes the point that it was ultimately the temple leaders who brought about the disaster of 70 C.E.

The image of a destroyed building, the temple, may have led Mark to add the quotation from one of the Psalms (118:22–23). Jesus questions his opponents: "Have you not read this scripture: 'The stone that the builders rejected has become the cornerstone; this was the Lord's doing, and it is amazing in our eyes'?" (12:10–11) A new structure will replace the old, one founded on Jesus. For Mark's readers it is another assurance that they are now God's people.

Jesus' principal opponents go down in defeat: "When they realized that he had told this parable against them, they wanted to arrest him, but they feared the crowd. So they left him and went away." (12:12) Their withdrawal is only temporary, of course. What they could not achieve by direct attack, they will achieve by duplicity.

2. THE PHARISEES AND HERODIANS

Having quit the field themselves, Jesus' main opponents now turn to allies. At the beginning of Jesus' public life, Mark notes: "The Pharisees went out and immediately conspired with the Herodians against him, how to destroy him." (3:6) Actually, neither of these groups had any role in determining the fate of Jesus. Here we have their final appearance wherein they pose a serious challenge to Jesus. Their attempt to trap him is preceded by oily compliments: "Teacher, we know that you are sincere, and show deference to no one; for you do not regard people with partiality, but teach the way of God in accordance with truth. Is it lawful to pay taxes to the emperor, or not? Should we pay them, or should we not?" (12:14–15)

Mark's readers would have had no difficulty appreciating the pit that opened at Jesus' feet. The Romans took the gathering of taxes very seriously. Any attempt to impede their collection was met with brutal force. On the other hand, taxes were even less popular in Mark's time than in ours. They were a heavy burden especially on the conquered peoples. Mark's Christians would have understood that Jesus' approval of their payment would alienate his listeners.

Jesus recognizes the hypocrisy of his questioners and asks to see a Roman coin: " 'Whose head is this, and whose title?' They answered, 'The emperor's.' Jesus said to them, 'Give to the emperor the things that are the emperor's, and to God the things that are God's.'" (12:17) Jesus' amazed challengers withdraw. Mark's readers could certainly appreciate the cleverness of Jesus' reply.

Did it go beyond that? These Christians had to pay taxes. Were they troubled by their contributions to support a pagan regime which they must have regarded as both idolatrous and immoral? If so, Jesus' reply may well have eased their consciences. It may have served another purpose as well. A Jesus who approved the payment of taxes could hardly have been regarded as a revolutionary threat.

3. THE SADDUCEES

The Sadducees, who now make their appearance, were the ruling class in Palestine and chief rivals of the Pharisees. The two sects differed sharply on the question of the resurrection of the dead, the Pharisees supporting the possibility and the Sadducees in opposition. We can assume that Mark's readers were familiar with the dispute and could appreciate the latter's confrontation with Jesus over the matter.

The Sadducees' question is an attempt at *reductio ad absurdum*. Under the *Levirite* law of Judaism (Deuteronomy 25:5–6) when a man dies childless, his brother shall marry the deceased man's wife and the first born of that union shall be considered the child of the man who died. Jesus' challengers then pose the case of this having happened to a woman seven times, so they ask, "In the resurrection whose wife will she be? For the seven had married her." (12:23)

Jesus replies that it is their premise which is absurd: "Is not this the reason you are wrong, that you know neither the scriptures nor the power of God? For when they rise from the dead, they neither marry nor are given in marriage, but are like angels in heaven. And as for the dead being raised, have you not read in the book of Moses, in the story about the bush, how God said to him, 'I am the God of Abraham, the God of Isaac, and the God of Jacob'? He is God not of the dead, but of the living; you are quite wrong." (12:25–27)

The Pharisees' hope for a resurrection of the dead was shared by Christians as we can see from Paul's writings. Here is but one example: "For if we have been united with [Jesus] in a death like his, we will certainly be united with him in a resurrection like his." (Romans 6:5) There was a similar expectation found among the mystery religions that were rivals of Christianity. "This victory [of the god] over death served as a promise to the adherents that [the cult members], too, could achieve immortality and a blessed life after death." (Jo-Ann Shelton, *op. cit.* p. 395) Jesus' reply would have hit a responsive chord among Mark's readers as well as others.

B. The Well–Intentioned Scribe

On this day of controversy, the final figure to appear in the temple is a scribe who we are told was impressed by Jesus' replies to his opponents. "One of the scribes came near and heard them disputing with one another, and seeing that [Jesus] answered them well, he asked him, 'Which commandment is the first of all?'" In reply, Jesus begins with a quote from Deuteronomy (6:4–5): "The first is, 'Hear, O Israel: the Lord our God, the Lord is one; you shall love the Lord your God with all your heart, and with all your soul, and with all your mind, and with all your strength.'" (12:29–30) To this Jesus adds, "The second is this, 'You shall love your neighbor as yourself.' There is no other commandment greater than these." (12:31) The addition is also to be found in the Hebrew Bible: "You shall not take vengeance or bear a grudge against any of your people, but you shall love your neighbor as yourself." (Leviticus 19:18) Jesus is unique in pairing these two quotations.

The scribe concurs with Jesus' response, and Jesus compliments the scribe in return: "'You are right, Teacher; you have truly said that 'he is one, and besides him there is no other'; and 'to love him with all the heart, and with all the understanding, and with all the strength,' and 'to love one's neighbor as oneself'—this is much more important than all whole burnt offerings and sacrifices.' When Jesus saw that he answered wisely, he said to him, 'You are not far from the kingdom of God.'" (12:32–34) It should be noted that Matthew and Luke, writing in times of increased hostility between Jew and Christian, omit this affable exchange between Jesus and the scribe.

C. Condemning the Scribes

The challenges to Jesus now end: "After that no one dared to ask him any question." (12:34) Mark continues on the subject of the scribes, now in less friendly terms. Jesus first disputes the scribal wisdom.

While Jesus was teaching in the temple, he said, "How can the scribes say that the Messiah is the son of David? David himself, by the Holy Spirit, declared, 'The Lord said to my Lord, "Sit at my right hand, until I put your enemies under your feet." ' David himself calls him Lord; so how can he be his son?" And the large crowd was listening to him with delight. (12:35–37)

When Jesus begins his climb from Jericho to Jerusalem he is recognized by the blind Bartimaeus as the "Son of David." (Mark 10:47–48) Mark is setting the scene for Jesus' triumphant entry into Jerusalem when the crowd accompanying Jesus cries out: "Blessed is the coming kingdom of our ancestor David! Hosanna in the highest heaven!" (11:10) Jesus is not so identified elsewhere in the first Gospel. The title would not have had much significance for Mark's Gentile community. Moreover, regal claims for Jesus would not have been politic in the period of the Jewish war.

Now in the above passage Mark seeks to undermine the very notion that the Messiah would be a descendant of David. "David himself calls [the Messiah] Lord; so how can he be his son?" Achtemeir wonders whether or not "the point of this story is to allow Jesus to claim to be the Christ even though he is not of the Davidic line (Matthew and Luke make it a point to include information that he is, but Mark contains no such traditions about Jesus' ancestry)...." (*Op. cit.* p. 43)

Mark's, Jesus, to the further delight of the crowd, follows with a very negative evaluation of the scribes: "Beware of the scribes, who like to walk around in long robes, and to be greeted with respect in the marketplaces, and to have the best seats in the synagogues and places of honor at banquets! They devour widows' houses and for the sake of appearance say long prayers. They will receive the greater condemnation." (12:38–40) Mark leaves his reader with a final, very negative, impression of Jesus' scribal opponents.

D. The Condemnation of the Temple

Mark's following scene can be seen as a transition from what he has to say about the scribes to what Jesus will foresee as the fate of the temple.

He sat down opposite the treasury, and watched the crowd putting money into the treasury. Many rich people put in large sums. A poor widow came and put in two small copper coins, which are worth a penny. Then he called his disciples and said to them, "Truly I tell you, this poor widow has put in more than all those who are contributing to the treasury. For all of them have contributed out of their abundance; but she out of her poverty has put in everything she had, all she had to live on." (12:41–44)

In spite of the usual interpretation, Mark is not praising the widow for her generosity but rather sees her impoverishment as an abuse, an echo of his condemnation of the scribes who "devour widows' houses." As we noted above, it is likely that Mark's readers saw a sample of the temple's glories paraded through the streets of Rome in the triumphal procession of Titus. Josephus made note of its wealth as well. (*Op. cit.* pp. 360, 368–369) Mark, who is about to bring to the reader's mind the temple's destruction, sees that fate justified in the poor widow's destitution.

Mark now makes his brief reference to the event that was quite vivid in the memory of his readers: "As [Jesus] came out of the temple, one of his disciples said to him, 'Look, Teacher, what large stones and what large buildings!' Then Jesus asked him, 'Do you see these great buildings? Not one stone will be left here upon another; all will be thrown down.'" (13:1–2) It is not impossible that members of Mark's community could have witnessed the fire that swept through the structure on that fateful day in 70 C.E. Others may have even seen the ruins.[7]

Whatever the case, it is the devastation of one of the ancient world's great architectural wonders that is the backdrop to Jesus' announcement of the approaching parousia. "When [Jesus] was sitting on the Mount of Olives opposite the temple, Peter, James, John, and Andrew asked him privately, 'Tell us, when will this be, and what will be the sign that all these things are about to be accomplished?'" (13:3–4) As noted earlier, the prophet Zechariah pictures God standing on the Mount of Olives on the day of his apocalyptic appearance (14:4). We have dealt with the following passages of Mark in great detail in an earlier chapter where the prediction of the parousia was discussed.

Mark sets the scene for the climactic events of Jesus' life by showing him moving from triumph to triumph. He enters the city of Jerusalem amidst a cheering crowd. Jesus drives the merchants and money changers from the temple. Then, in the temple precincts, he sends his opponents, one by one, away in defeat. Finally, recalling to the reader's mind the fate of the temple, Mark has Jesus announce his return "with great power and glory." (13:26) For the first readers of Mark's Gospel, the parousia was not lost in a dim future, but was soon to occur. "Truly I tell you, this generation will not pass away until all these things have taken place." (13:30)

The mood of events is to change. Now the account of Jesus' final days will move from triumphs to a crushing defeat. There will be no appearance of a risen Lord in Mark as there is in the Gospels of his successors.[8] Mark's readers look forward to Jesus' final triumph when he returns at the parousia. That hope sustains them as the Gospel moves to betrayal, condemnation and execution.

STUDY QUESTIONS

1. In its final chapters changes take place in the style of the first Gospel. What are they?
2. What might have been the reason for these changes?
3. Why were the final events of Jesus' life arranged over a seven-day cycle?
4. What is unusual about Jesus' encounter with Bartimaeus?
5. Whose prophecy is prominent in the Marcan account of Jesus' entry into Jerusalem?
6. What is significant about Jesus' cursing the fig tree?
7. Why would Jesus' cleansing of the temple have a special meaning for Mark's community?
8. What did the withering of the fig tree foreshadow?
9. On the "day of controversies" who are the real enemies of Jesus?
10. How does Jesus meet their challenge?
11. In what manner do the Pharisees and Herodians seek to trap Jesus?
12. How did the Sadducees challenge Jesus?
13. What is unusual about the exchange between Jesus and the scribe?
14. In what way does Jesus attack the scribes as a group?
15. What is the significance of the poor widow?
16. With what prophecy does Jesus close the "day of controversy"?

Chapter Twelve

THE HOLY WEEK
PART TWO: WEDNESDAY
AND THURSDAY

I. THE DAY OF MERCURY

Now, for Mark's readers, the plot against Jesus intensifies. "It was two days,[1] before the Passover and the festival of Unleavened Bread. The chief priests and the scribes were looking for a way to arrest Jesus by stealth and kill him; for they said, 'Not during the festival, or there may be a riot among the people.'" (14:1–2) The solution to their problem will shortly be offered to them by Judas. Now, before that happens, Mark recounts a scene that contrasts with the plot by Jesus' enemies and his betrayal by one of his own.

Seemingly oblivious to the growing threat, Mark's Jesus spends the day not far from Jerusalem, with his close associates: "While he was at Bethany in the house of Simon the leper, as he sat at the table, a woman came with an alabaster jar of very costly ointment of nard, and she broke open the jar and poured the ointment on his head." (14:3). Hers is an implicit testimony to Jesus as the "Anointed," the Messiah.

There are those present who miss the point and complain, "Why was the ointment wasted in this way? For this ointment could have been sold for more than three hundred denarii, and the money given to the poor." (14:4–5) Could Mark be anticipating his own readers' objections in Jesus' reply? "Let her alone; why do you trouble her? She has performed a good service for me. For you always have the poor with you, and you can show kindness to them whenever you wish; but you will not always have me." (14:6–7) The woman's "good service" foresees what is to come. "She has anointed my body beforehand for its

136

burial." (14:8) The customary preparations for entombment will be omitted after Jesus' death. Supplying them will bring the women to the tomb on Easter Sunday morning.

The reference to the anointing of Jesus' body after his suffering and death links that death to his title as Messiah. Here, then, we have an expression of the Marcan theme of Jesus as the suffering Messiah. As we saw earlier, Peter and the apostles had failed to understand this. In contrast, the woman's "good service" gives expression to it. For her action the unidentified woman will be forever remembered: "Truly I tell you, wherever the good news is proclaimed in the whole world, what she has done will be told in remembrance of her." (14:9)

Now is initiated the chain of events that will bring Jesus to his death. An apostle betrays Jesus. "Then Judas Iscariot, who was one of the twelve, went to the chief priests in order to betray him to them. When they heard it, they were greatly pleased, and promised to give him money. So he began to look for an opportunity to betray him." (14:10–11) There is an irony here; Judas, like the woman at Simon's, will also be forever remembered in the Good News, he for his betrayal, she for her kindness.

II. THE DAY OF JUPITER

A. The Passover Meal

> With sunset of the following day, the feast of Passover will begin. On the first day of Unleavened Bread, when the Passover lamb is sacrificed, his disciples said to him, "Where do you want us to go and make the preparations for you to eat the Passover?" So he sent two of his disciples, saying to them, "Go into the city, and a man carrying a jar of water will meet you; follow him, and wherever he enters, say to the owner of the house, 'The Teacher asks, Where is my guest room where I may eat the Passover with my disciples?' He will show you a large room upstairs, furnished and ready. Make preparations for us there." (14:12–15)

In the scene that follows, Mark gives no details reflecting the traditional Jewish seder meal. Moreover, the conduct of the chief priests in the coming hours is quite contrary to what was permitted behavior on so solemn a feast day.[2] Quite possibly, neither of these details would have been noticed by Mark's Gentile readers. What Mark emphasizes at the beginning is that Jesus knows the identity of his betrayer: "When it was evening, he came with the twelve. And when they had taken their places and were eating, Jesus said, 'Truly I tell you, one of you will betray me, one who is eating with me.' They began to be distressed and to say to him one after another, 'Surely, not I?' He said to them, 'It is one of the twelve, one who is dipping bread into the bowl with me.'" (14:17–20)

Jesus conceals the identity of the culprit, thus freeing him to carry out his plot. Why? Mark wants to make it clear that Jesus could have at any time escaped his fate. Jesus does not because he must fulfill his destiny: "For the Son of Man goes as it is written of him." (14:21) Mark gives the reader the portrait of one stoically and deliberately going to his fate, fully conscious of what it is. Though Judas is the pawn, as it were, of destiny, he does not escape blame. "Woe to that one by whom the Son of Man is betrayed! It would have been better for that one not to have been born." (14:21)

B. The Eucharist

We saw earlier that the celebration of the "Lord's supper" was central to the gatherings of both the house and the local Pauline churches. We can presume that the same was true for the Marcan community. Like Paul, Mark has Jesus originate the eucharist "on the night when he was betrayed." (I Corinthians 11:23; Mark 14:22–24) Fredriksen asks: "Did [Jesus] then specifically associate the bread and wine of the meal with his own body and blood, and these with the eschatological ... covenant? Again, we cannot be certain; but the early Christian communities certainly did, as they too celebrated by eating together in anticipation of a Messianic banquet that would signify not their messiah's arrival, but his return in glory." (*Ibid.* p. 115) Given what has been said, Mark's Christians would have celebrated with just such an anticipation.

In Mark, Jesus says, "Truly I tell you, I will never again drink of the fruit of the vine until that day when I drink it new in the kingdom of God." (14:25) When they celebrated the eucharist, Mark's church would have expected to soon be joining with Jesus in that ultimate banquet which characterizes the parousia.

C. The Betrayal

The Passover meal ends. "When they had sung the hymn, they went out to the Mount of Olives." (14:26) The reference is not necessarily to singing as part of the Jewish Passover service but rather is to the Christians' own practice of singing at celebrations (see Colossians 3:16; Ephesians 5:19). Raymond Brown comments: "Mark's first readers/hearers (even as readers today) would have thought of hymn(s)-singing familiar to them without reflecting about the historical situation many years before." (*The Death of the Messiah*, p. 123)

We have come full circle. It was from here that Jesus and his disciples entered the holy city on the first day of his final week (11:1) and it was while on the Mount of Olives that Jesus told his followers of the signs that would announce the parousia (13:3). Now, as the moment of crisis nears, Jesus has returned to the mount to make a dread announcement: "You will all become deserters; for it is written, 'I will strike the shepherd, and the sheep will be scattered.'" (14:27) In Mark's account of Jesus' suffering and death only here does the evangelist make an explicit citation of Scripture (Zechariah 13:7) Yet, there may be another memory brought to mind here. David, fleeing from his betrayal by his son Absolom, "went up the ascent of the Mount of Olives, weeping as he went." (II Samuel 15:30) Jesus will soon be betrayed and deserted by those closest to him.

Jesus continues: "But after I am raised up, I will go before you to Galilee." (14:28) Mark is preparing the reader for the final lines of the Gospel. The women at the tomb are told, "But go, tell his disciples and Peter that he is going ahead of you to Galilee; there you will see him, just as he told you." (16:7) Jesus' followers are to be scattered, yes, but they will be gathered together once again.

Mark also lays the groundwork for another scene to come. When Peter protests, "Even though all become deserters, I will not" (14:29), Jesus replies, "Truly I tell you, this day, this very night, before the cock crows twice, you will deny me three times." (14:30) Peter persists, "Even though I must die with you, I will not deny you." (14:31) It is a hollow boast that prepares the reader for the final embarrassment of the apostolic leader.

The group of Jesus and his followers proceed farther. "They went to a place called Gethsemani; and he said to his disciples, 'Sit here while I pray.' He took with him Peter and James and John, and began to be distressed and agitated." (14:32–33) Jesus' selection of these three from the rest has occurred before, once to witness his deed of power in curing the daughter of Jairus (5:37) and again for them to be present at his transfiguration (9:2).

How different is what these three now witness! "Distressed and agitated," Jesus tells them, "I am deeply grieved, even to death." (14:34) The power and transcendence that revealed Jesus' divinity are replaced by the anguish that makes clear his humanity. The one who was seen as so mighty is now seen as so weak. Is this the challenge that Jesus' disciples really failed? Raymond Brown observes, "Besides portraying Jesus' own struggle in the face of evil, Mark shows that the best-known disciples never understood either Jesus' glory or his anguish." (*Op. cit.* p. 152)

Up to now, Mark has presented Jesus as one calmly, even stoically, facing the fate that awaits him. Abruptly, the mood changes. Jesus "threw himself on the ground and prayed that, if it were possible, the hour might pass from him. He said, 'Abba, Father, for you all things are possible; remove this cup from me; yet, not what I want, but what you want.'" (14:35–36) Faced with the ultimate trial, Jesus displays his humanity by shrinking back, hoping to be spared. His plea is made all the more poignant by Jesus' use of the childlike "Abba," an appellation similar to "Daddy" in English.

It is a scene not without meaning for Mark's readers. The coming parousia will be a time of testing for them. "As Mark's readers face their trial and find it too much, emboldened by knowing that all things are possible with God, they may find themselves, despite all their previous commitments, asking that this cup may be taken away. And they can do that in Jesus' name provided that they add as he did, 'But not what I will but what you [will].'" (Brown, *ibid.* p. 178)

Jesus' determination to do his Father's will is contrasted with yet another failure on the part of his disciples. They are unable to stay awake. "[Jesus] came and found them sleeping; and he said to Peter, 'Simon, are you asleep? Could you not keep awake one hour? Keep awake and pray that you may not come into the time of trial; the spirit indeed is willing, but the flesh is weak.'" (14:37–38) Jesus' admonition may be seen as a warning to the reader, echoing the earlier, "Therefore, keep awake—for you do not know when the master of the house will come, in the evening, or at midnight, or at cockcrow, or at dawn, or else he may find you asleep when he comes suddenly. And what I say to you I say to all: 'Keep awake.'" (13:35–37) They must not be caught unawares as were Jesus' own disciples.

Now it is too late: "Are you still sleeping and taking your rest? Enough! The hour has come; the Son of Man is betrayed into the hands of sinners. Get up, let us be going. See, my betrayer is at hand." (14:41–42) Though aware of the threat about to be realized, Jesus makes no attempt to escape. "Immediately, while [Jesus] was still speaking, Judas, one of the twelve, arrived; and with him there was a crowd with swords and clubs, from the chief priests, the scribes, and the elders. Now the betrayer had given them a sign, saying, 'The one I will kiss is the man; arrest him and lead him away under guard.' So when he came, he went up to him at once and said, 'Rabbi!' and kissed him." (14:43–45)

It is just as Jesus had predicted: "The Son of Man is to be betrayed into human hands." (9:31) The kiss was a mark of respect, even friendship, as it still is in many cultures. The enormity of the act of betraying with a kiss would not have been lost on Mark's readers. Jesus himself points out the basic cowardice of his arrest by such force, at night and in a remote place. "Have you come out with swords and clubs to arrest me as though I were a bandit? Day after day I was with you in the temple teaching, and you did not arrest me. But let the scriptures be fulfilled." (14:48–49) Again what happens occurs because Jesus is determined to fulfill the will of God.

"All of [Jesus' followers] deserted him and fled.[3] A certain young man was following him, wearing nothing but a linen cloth. They caught hold of him, but he left the linen cloth and ran off naked." (14:50–52) The lone figure fleeing naked has been the subject of much speculation, some even positing that it was the author of the Gospel.

What is more likely is that Mark sought to emphasize the panic of Jesus' deserting disciples. One even scurries away stripped of his clothing. Such is the final touch Mark gives to his negative portrayal of the disciples.

D. The Trial before the High Priest

As we know little of the Jewish legal procedures in force early in the first century, we cannot judge how accurately Mark has recounted the trial and condemnation of Jesus. In this connection, Fredriksen observes: "If we relinquish the effort to see the Sanhedrin trial as history, we can receive more clearly the theological effect it achieves." (*Op. cit.* p. 117) Mark's interest is not so much to tell his reader what actually happened, but rather to further apprise the reader of who Jesus is.

He stands before his enemies and at their mercy. "They took Jesus to the high priest; and all the chief priests, the elders, and the scribes were assembled." (14:53) Later this group will be referred to as "the chief priests and the whole council."[4] (14:55) Mark may have had in mind the same body Josephus refers to as "the chief priests and the Sanhedrin." (*Op. cit.* pp. 154,155) Whether such a formally organized group existed in Jesus' time is not known.

The trial itself is a farce:

> Now the chief priests and the whole council were looking for testimony against Jesus to put him to death; but they found none. For many gave false testimony against him, and their testimony did not agree. Some stood up and gave false testimony against him, saying, "We heard him say, 'I will destroy this temple that is made with hands, and in three days I will build another, not made with hands.'" But even on this point their testimony did not agree. (14:55–59)

The false testimony is ironic. When the Gospel is being written the temple "made with human hands" has already been destroyed. As Brown remarks: "What replaces the empty sanctuary of the Jerusalem temple as the holy place of God is a community of believers...." (*Ibid.* p. 453) Mark's church is the "temple ... not made with hands." Here Mark may be mirroring the imagery of Paul: "Do you not know that you are God's temple? ... For God's temple is holy, and you are that temple." (I Corinthians 3:16, 17; see also 6:19; II Corinthians 6:16)

Now we come to the crucial juncture of the trial: "Then the high priest stood up before them and asked Jesus, 'Have you no answer? What is it that they testify against you?' But he was silent and did not answer. Again the high priest asked him, 'Are you the Messiah, the Son of the Blessed One?'" (14:60–61) Mark has already answered the question. The opening words of the Gospel were, "The beginning of the good news of Jesus Christ, the Son of God." (1:1) As Fredriksen notes: "The query the High Priest is made to utter—'are you the Christ, the Son of the Blessed?'—is precisely the Christian confession. Jesus *is* the Christ, he *is* the Son of God, and so he is presented here, in effect, dying for Christianity." (*Ibid.* p. 117) Again, the irony would not have been lost on Mark's readers.

In his reply, Jesus accepts the titles accorded him by the high priest and he couples them with a third: "I am; and 'you will see the Son of Man seated at the right hand of the Power,' and 'coming with the clouds of heaven.'" (14:62) Mark brings to the reader's mind Scripture passages referred to earlier: "The LORD says to my lord, Sit at my right hand until I make your enemies your footstool" (Psalm 110:1), "As I watched in the night visions, I saw one like a human being coming with the clouds of heaven." (Daniel 7:13) As he did at Caesarea Philippi (8:27,31) Mark links Jesus as the Messiah with Jesus as the Son of Man. The coming sufferings of Jesus will lead to his triumphant return at the parousia.

Mark makes clear to his readers that it is for these affirmations that Jesus is sent to his death. "Then the high priest tore his clothes[5] and said, 'Why do we still need witnesses? You have heard his blasphemy! What is your decision?' All of them condemned him as deserving death." (14:63–64) The charge of blasphemy had been raised before, on the occasion when Jesus assured the paralytic that his sins were forgiven. Scribes protest: "Why does this fellow speak in this way? It is blasphemy! Who can forgive sins but God alone?" (2:7) Mark's readers would have certainly known that their belief in Jesus' divinity was regarded as blasphemy by the Jews.

Jesus' sufferings begin immediately. "Some began to spit on him, to blindfold him, and to strike him, saying to him, 'Prophesy!' The guards also took him over and beat him." (14:65) Brown sees here a cruel version of a children's game: "There is a good possibility, in my judgment, that the Marcan phrase about covering the face is quite intelligible in the light of a game that would have been known to the readers." (*Ibid.* p. 574) A blindfolded child is asked to guess who slapped him.

We may have another example of the author's irony. The reader is reminded of Isaiah's words: "I did not hide my face from insult and spitting.... I know that I shall not be put to shame." (50:6,7) As Jesus' enemies mock him as a false prophet they fulfill a prophecy, "the great Isaian prophecy revealing that by self-giving a victim can turn the signs of human rejection into victory through God's help." (Brown, *ibid.* p. 577) And the irony is reinforced. In the scene that follows, Jesus is shown to be a quite accurate prophet.

Juxtaposed with Jesus' being condemned and abused, Mark places the ultimate humiliation of the apostolic leader. Before the above scene began, Peter had been placed nearby. "Peter had followed [Jesus] at a distance, right into the courtyard of the high priest; and he was sitting with the guards, warming himself at the fire." (14:55) Jesus' own prediction is about to be fulfilled: "Truly I tell you [Peter], this day, this very night, before the cock crows twice, you will deny me three times." (14:30)

"One of the servant-girls of the high priest came by. When she saw Peter warming himself, she stared at him and said, 'You also were with Jesus, the man from Nazareth.' But he denied it, saying, 'I do not know or understand what you are talking about.'" (14:66–68) As Peter flees to the forecourt, the cock crows.[6] Pursued by the servant-girl, Peter again denies any knowledge of Jesus. Now the bystanders take up the accusation: "Certainly you are one of them; for you are a Galilean." (14:70) Betrayed, probably by his speech, Peter "began to curse, and he swore an oath, 'I do not know this man you are talking about.'" (14:71) As he lies under oath in his denial of Jesus, the second cock crow is heard. With this, Peter recalls Jesus' prediction, "And he broke down and wept." (14:72) Mark does at least accord the leader of the apostles the mercy of penitence.

In the eyes of the reader, Jesus now stands betrayed, condemned, abused and deserted. As Jesus' passion begins Mark may have wished to bring to the reader's mind the "suffering servant" of Isaiah. Four passages from Isaiah make reference to a servant of God who suffers unjustly.[7] Scholars debate whom they refer to. However, the early Christians saw in them a reference to Jesus. "He was despised and rejected by others; a man of suffering and acquainted with infirmity; and as one from whom others hide their faces he was despised, and we held him of no account.... By a perversion of justice he was taken away." (53:3,8) It is a very human Jesus who will now appear before Pontius Pilate, the Roman procurator.

STUDY QUESTIONS

1. What is the meaning behind Jesus being anointed in the house of Simon the Leper?
2. Jesus knows his betrayer yet does nothing to escape. Why?
3. Would the Lord's Supper have had a special meaning for Mark's community?
4. On three occasions, Jesus comes to the Mount of Olives. How does the final scene contrast with the first two?
5. What is particularly striking about Jesus' prayer to his Father?
6. How are Jesus' disciples, especially Peter, made to appear in this scene?
7. What might be the explanation for the young man's fleeing naked?
8. What is the irony in the charge brought against Jesus?
9. What is the question the high priest asks Jesus?
10. What passages from the Hebrew Bible are reflected in the descriptions of Jesus' sufferings?
11. What might lie behind Jesus' abuse by the guards?
12. How does Jesus appear to the reader as his first trial ends?

Chapter Thirteen

THE HOLY WEEK
PART THREE: FRIDAY TO SUNDAY

I. THE DAY OF VENUS

A. *The Trial before Pilate*

Speaking of the Christians, Tacitus wrote, "Their originator, Christ, had been executed in Tiberius' reign by the governor of Judea, Pontius Pilate." (*Annals,* p. 365) Mark had to face the fact that Jesus of Nazareth had been put to death by a Roman authority. "As soon as it was morning the chief priests held a consultation with the elders and scribes and the whole council. They bound Jesus, led him away, and handed him over to Pilate." (15:1) However, the charge against Jesus now is not his claim to be "the Messiah, the Son of the Blessed One." (14:61) The reader is told, "Pilate asked him, 'Are you the King of the Jews?'" (15:2)

The matter is delicate. Rome had just recently ended a long and costly war caused by Jewish claims to independence. The accusation that Jesus had been a pretender to the crown of Israel must have been of acute embarrassment to the Christians. As noted earlier, Mark specifically denies that the Messiah was of Davidic descent. (12:35–37) Nor does Jesus ever make any such claim of royalty. Though Mark certainly believed the charge to be false, Jesus' reply to Pilate, "You say so" (15:2), seems ambiguous. To confuse the procurator the more, Jesus then "stands mute."

"Then the chief priests accused him of many things. Pilate asked him again, 'Have you no answer? See how many charges they bring against you.' But Jesus made no further reply, so that Pilate was amazed." (15:3–5) In this silence of Jesus Mark may again be reminding his readers of the Isaian suffering servant of God: "He was oppressed, and he was afflicted, yet he did not open his mouth." (53:7) Pilate's amazement also echoes Isaiah: "So he shall startle many nations; kings shall shut their mouths because of him." (52:15)

Mark now describes a custom for which we have no other historical confirmation: "At the festival [Pilate] used to release a prisoner for them, anyone for whom they asked. Now a man called Barabbas[1] was in prison with the rebels who had committed murder during the insurrection." (15:7) Given the Romans' recent bloody struggle putting down a rebellion in Palestine, Barabbas would have been regarded as the worst sort of criminal. He was what Jesus was not, and Mark certainly intends the contrast.

"So the crowd came and began to ask Pilate to do for them according to his custom." (15:8) Mark can now make it clear that even Pilate was convinced of Jesus' innocence. The procurator asks the crowd, "Do you want me to release for you the King of the Jews?" (15:9) Pilate "realized that it was out of jealousy that the chief priests had handed [Jesus] over." (15:10) But Pilate's ploy is frustrated, for "the chief priests stirred up the crowd to have him release Barabbas for them instead." (15:11) With this Mark adds another touch to his negative portrait of Jesus' enemies. In their zeal to destroy Jesus they engineered the freedom of an actual insurgent, one who was a murderer as well.

In the end, it is not Pilate who passes sentence on Jesus. Pilate asks the crowd, "What do you wish me to do with the man you call the King of the Jews?" (15:12) It is the crowd that determines Jesus' fate: "They shouted back, 'Crucify him!' Pilate asked them, 'Why, what evil has he done?' But they shouted all the more, 'Crucify him!'" (15:13–14) Mark could hardly have made it any clearer that it was the chief priests and their cohort who brought about a grave miscarriage of justice. The procurator can only unwillingly acquiesce to their demands. "So Pilate, wishing to satisfy the crowd, released Barabbas for them; and after flogging[2] Jesus, he handed him over to be crucified." (15:15)

B. *The Crucifixion of Jesus*

1. THE MOCKERY

In the scene that follows, Mark seems to be showing just how ridiculous it was to see Jesus as the "King of the Jews." The readers would have seen the emperor, clad in royal purple, wearing the golden diadem, receiving the praise of cheering subjects. Look, the evangelist is saying, at the sort of king Jesus was:

> Then the soldiers led him into the courtyard of the palace (that is, the governor's headquarters); and they called together the whole cohort. And they clothed him in a purple cloak; and after twisting some thorns into a crown, they put it on him. And they began saluting him, "Hail, King of the Jews!"[3] They struck his head with a reed, spat upon him, and knelt down in homage to him. After mocking him, they stripped him of the purple cloak and put his own clothes on him. Then they led him out to crucify him. (15:16–20)

Brown notes (*op. cit.* p. 877) that the two mockeries, one by the Jews and one by the Romans, reflect the duality found in Paul's "We proclaim Christ crucified, a stumbling block to Jews and foolishness to Gentiles." (I Corinthians 1:23) There is irony here. Jesus, mocked as a prophet, proved to be prophetic. Now he is mocked as a king. Mark's readers, expecting the coming of God's kingdom, know Jesus will soon prove to be regal as well. Also, in this vivid scene of Jesus being degraded and abused, Mark recalls again the "suffering servant" passages found in Isaiah: "I gave my back to those who struck me, and my cheeks to those who pulled out the beard; I did not hide my face from insult and spitting." (50:6)

We noted earlier that a victim being driven through the street on the way to his crucifixion was an all too common sight for Mark's readers. The unfortunate would have stumbled under the weight of the beam that was to become his means of execution. Mark may be adding here an element of the actual event. "[The soldiers] compelled a passerby, who was coming in from the country, to carry his cross;[4] it was Simon of Cyrene, the father of Alexander and Rufus." (15:21) As Brown observes, "Thus there is no inherent implausibility that there could have been a Cyrenian Jew named Simon in Jerusalem at the time of

Jesus' death and that he could have become a Christian." (*Ibid.* p. 915) The assumption is that his sons, Alexander and Rufus, were known to Mark's community. Paul, in writing to Rome, does greet a "Rufus" (16:13), possibly the same. We can speculate that there may have been a living link between some of Mark's readers and the final hours of Jesus' life.

2. THE EXECUTION

Mark's description of the crucifixion is brief and precise. He had no need to go into the details of what was for Christians a painful memory and, as we have said, a familiar sight.

> Then they brought Jesus to the place called Golgotha (which means the place of a skull[5]). And they offered him wine mixed with myrrh; but he did not take it. And they crucified him,[6] and divided his clothes among them, casting lots to decide what each should take. It was nine o'clock in the morning when they crucified him. The inscription of the charge against him read, "The King of the Jews." And with him they crucified two bandits, one on his right and one on his left. (15:22–27)

Though stark, the details of Jesus' execution given in Mark have the ring of authenticity. Victims of crucifixion were offered a drink to deaden their agony to some measure. The victim's clothing became the property of his executioners. Some indication of the charge for which the victim was being punished was usually displayed. Multiple executions at a single site were also common. On the other hand, Mark's indication of the times, crucifixion at nine in the morning, darkness at noon (15:33), death at three (15:34) and burial as evening approaches (15:42) is probably artificial.[7] It has been suggested that these might reflect the hour of prayer for Mark's community. (Cf. Brown, *ibid.* p. 960)

There also may have been symbolic aspects of the details Mark cites. In refusing what would lessen his suffering, Jesus shows his determination to drink the cup the Father has given him. Then Psalm 22 would come to the reader's mind: "They divide my clothes among themselves, and for my clothing they cast lots." (v. 18) As we will see, this Psalm was particularly influential in the formation of the passion narrative in Mark. Finally, we would have Isaiah's prophecy of the "suffering servant" who was "numbered with the transgressors." (53:12)

3. JESUS ON THE CROSS

Now three groups mock Jesus as he hangs on the cross. First there are the passersby who "derided him, shaking their heads and saying, 'Aha! You who would destroy the temple and build it in three days, save yourself, and come down from the cross!'" (15:29–30) Could the irony here be lost on Mark's readers? The temple has been destroyed. They have seen its looted treasures carried through Rome. Yet, Jesus rose from the dead and is expected to return shortly in triumph. We also have another echo of Psalm 22: "All who see me mock at me; they make mouths at me, they shake their head." (v. 7)

Next it is the turn of Jesus' seemingly victorious enemies: "In the same way the chief priests, along with the scribes, were also mocking him among themselves and saying, 'He saved others; he cannot save himself. Let the Messiah, the King of Israel, come down from the cross now, so that we may see and believe.'" (15:31–32) Nevertheless, their victory is hollow. The reader knows their successors have been destroyed along with the temple. It is Jesus who has conquered. Again, there is a resonance of Psalm 22: "Commit your cause to the LORD; let him deliver—let him rescue the one in whom he delights!" (v. 8)

Finally, even the wretches crucified with Jesus join in the mockery. "Those who were crucified with him also taunted him." (15:32) There is no hint here of Luke's "good thief"; Mark's depiction is unrelievably bleak. Jesus is now completely abandoned. The words of the Psalmist are fulfilled: "But I am a worm, and not human; scorned by others, and despised by the people." (22:6) The climactic moment is at hand.

4. THE DEATH OF JESUS

Mark sets the scene: "When it was noon, darkness came over the whole land until three in the afternoon." (15:33) The evangelist calls to the reader's mind the prophecy of Amos: "On that day, says the Lord GOD, I will make the sun go down at noon, and darken the earth in broad daylight. I will turn your feasts into mourning, and all your songs into lamentation; I will bring sackcloth on all loins, and baldness on every head; I will make it like the mourning for an only son, and the end of it like a bitter day." (8:9–10) The one who is to die now is both "Son of God" and "Son of Man." The darkness at noon gives an eschatological significance to what is about to happen. For Mark's Romans there was also the memory that at the death of Julius Caesar the light of the sun was darkened.

"At three o'clock Jesus cried out with a loud voice, 'Eloi, Eloi, lema sabachthani?' which means, 'My God, my God, why have you forsaken me?'" (15:34) Can we take these words literally? Brown answers in the affirmative: "If one accepts literally that anguish at the opening moment when Jesus could still call God 'Abba, Father,' one should accept equally the literally screamed protest against abandonment wrenched from an utterly forlorn Jesus who is now so isolated and estranged that he no longer uses 'Father' language but speaks as the humblest servant." (Ibid. p. 1051) From such a perspective, we would have Mark's most convincing evidence for Jesus' humanity. The effect is made all the more vivid by Mark's use of what his readers would have taken for Jesus' own words in Aramaic, Eloi, Eloi, lema sabachthani.

Nevertheless, Brown admits: "While I find this interpretation of Mark convincing, in fairness it should be noted that from the early Church Fathers to contemporary scholars and preachers many have resisted the surface import that would have Jesus expressing the sentiment of being forsaken by God." (Ibid. p. 1047) The reality of Jesus' humanity has been a challenge for Christians from the beginning as it is still. On the other hand, there have been those who found his humanity a comfort, as we read in Hebrews: "For we do not have a high priest who is unable to sympathize with our weaknesses, but we have one who in every respect has been tested as we are, yet without sin." (4:15)

One way of dealing with the challenge is to understand Jesus' cry in the light of the whole of Psalm 22 of which "My God, my God, why have you forsaken me?" is the opening line. As we have seen the Psalm is reflected in Mark's representation of Jesus' suffering:

> But I am a worm, and not human; scorned by others, and despised by the people. All who see me mock at me; they make mouths at me, they shake their heads; "Commit your cause to the LORD; let him deliver—let him rescue the one in whom he delights!"... I am poured out like water, and all my bones are out of joint; my heart is like wax; it is

melted within my breast; my mouth is dried up like a potsherd, and my
tongue sticks to my jaws; you lay me in the dust of death. For dogs are
all around me; a company of evildoers encircles me. My hands and feet
have shriveled; I can count all my bones. They stare and gloat over me;
they divide my clothes among themselves, and for my clothing they
cast lots. (vv. 6–8,14–18)

There is a note of despair in the Psalm as it continues: "Why are
you so far from helping me, from the words of my groaning? O my
God, I cry by day, but you do not answer; and by night, but find no
rest." (22:1–2) Yet, lack of hope is really not the theme of the Psalm;
rather it is one of trust conquering despair: "But you, O LORD, do not
be far away! O my help, come quickly to my aid! Deliver my soul
from the sword, my life from the power of the dog! ... For [the
LORD] did not despise or abhor the affliction of the afflicted; he did
not hide his face from me, but heard when I cried to him."
(22:19–20,24) The Psalm concludes praising God: "Posterity will
serve him; future generations will be told about the Lord, and proclaim
his deliverance to a people yet unborn, saying that he has done it."
(22:30–31) Mark's readers would certainly have seen themselves as
the "people yet unborn." The hope expressed in the Psalm is not just
that of Jesus, it is also the hope of Mark's Christians. By recalling
Psalm 22 as a whole the element of despair is softened in Jesus' words
from the cross.

All of this is lost on the onlookers, some of whom mistake Jesus'
cry, "Eloi,"[8] for Elijah: "When some of the bystanders heard it, they
said, 'Listen, he is calling for Elijah.' And someone ran, filled a sponge
with sour wine, put it on a stick, and gave it to him to drink, saying,
'Wait, let us see whether Elijah will come to take him down.'"
(15:35–36) Why the mention of Elijah? Brown observes: "Elijah was
very prominent in the popular expectation of the endtimes, as miracle
worker in time of mortal need, as forerunner of God's coming, as
anointer of the Messiah." (Ibid. p. 1062) Thus we have another
instance of Jesus being mocked by his tormentors.

The note of mockery is reinforced by the offer of sour wine.[9] Mark
recalls for the reader Psalm 69. It the plea for God's help: "I am weary
with my crying; my throat is parched. My eyes grow dim with waiting

for my God." (v. 3) But the psalmist's enemies only make matters worse: "They gave me poison for food, and for my thirst they gave me vinegar to drink." (v. 21) Yet, as with Psalm 22, we have the note of hope: "For the LORD hears the needy, and does not despise his own that are in bonds." (v. 33)

The climactic moment is brief. "Then Jesus gave a loud cry and breathed his last. And the curtain of the temple was torn in two, from top to bottom." (15:37–38) The simultaneity is important. The scream, the last breath and the tearing of the temple's curtain are to be superimposed in the mind's eye of the reader. "By the violent rending (*schizein*) God responds vigorously, not only to vindicate Jesus whom God has *not* forsaken but also to express anger at the chief priests who decreed such a death for God's Son." (Brown, *ibid.* p. 1100) The symbolism goes further. "Against the background of the sanctuary as a divine dwelling place—an idea shared by pagans and Jews alike—rending the veil could mean that the deity or the deity's presence had left." (*Ibid.* p. 1101) Mark's community knew the full meaning of the sign for the temple had just been destroyed entirely.

These Christians would have had a vivid reminder of the disaster. Josephus notes that among the treasures saved from the burning temple were its opulent hangings. (*Op. cit.* p. 369) These same curtains were carried in triumph through the streets of the capital as part of Vespasian's and Titus' booty brought back from Jerusalem. "There were hangings borne along, some in rarest shades of purple...." (*Ibid.* p. 384) It would be quite likely that members of Mark's community and, perhaps, the writer himself saw this procession. It must have forcibly brought home to Mark's community the full impact of the temple's destruction. It is easy to see why these Christians would now expect Jesus himself to return in power.

5. THE CENTURION

To the death of Jesus, Mark introduces a witness: "Now when the centurion, who stood facing him, saw that in this way he breathed his last, he said, 'Truly this man was God's Son!'" (15:39) He saw what the reader saw and then he expresses the faith of the reader. In Mark's Gospel, the centurion is the sole human being to understand that Jesus was the Son of God. And he comes to that understanding when, by normal standards, Jesus appears the least God-like; he is hanging lifeless on a cross. Also, like Mark's readers, the centurion was no doubt a Gentile. There is more to recommend the centurion as the crucial witness of Jesus' death. Rome had always harked back to its origins as a militarized community of citizen soldiers. The basic unit of that society was always the "100" and the basic military rank, the centurion. Thus there was a particularly Roman aura to the centurion. Was there something else at work here? The sect of Mithraism, an early rival to Christianity and open only to men, was particularly prevalent among the military. Was Mark seeking to increase Christianity's appeal to the same group?

Mark now adds to the scene another group of witnesses: "There were also women looking on from a distance; among them were Mary Magdalene, and Mary the mother of James the younger and of Joses, and Salome." (15:40) As Mark had never mentioned women in Jesus' entourage before, he adds a bit of background: "These used to follow him and provided for him when he was in Galilee; and there were many other women who had come up with him to Jerusalem." (15:41) Though the reader knows nothing more about them, they are to play a crucial role as Mark brings his Gospel to a close.

C. The Burial of Jesus

"When evening had come, and since it was the day of Preparation, that is, the day before the sabbath, Joseph of Arimathea, a respected member of the council, who was also himself waiting expectantly for the kingdom of God, went boldly to Pilate and asked for the body of Jesus." (15:41–43) There is no indication that Joseph was himself a follower of Jesus. Mark's readers would have been aware of the Jewish sensitivity over a body being left so exposed, especially on the sabbath. Joseph's initiative was the action of a pious Jew. Aware of the Roman sensitivity to even a hint of treason, the reader would have also appreciated what courage Joseph displayed.

Joseph's request enables Mark to establish another point: "Then Pilate wondered if he were already dead; and summoning the centurion, he asked him whether he had been dead for some time. When he learned from the centurion that he was dead, he granted the body to Joseph."

(15:44–45) Note who give testimony to Jesus' being dead: a Jew from the Sanhedrin, a Roman centurion and the Roman governor, Pilate. If there was a rumor that Jesus was only in a coma when taken down from the cross, Mark has done what he could to disprove the charge.

The burial is simple with the minimum of amenities: "Then Joseph bought a linen cloth, and taking down the body, wrapped it in the linen cloth, and laid it in a tomb that had been hewn out of the rock. He then rolled a stone against the door of the tomb." (15:46) As the Roman manner of burial was preceded by cremation, Mark's account of Jesus' entombment reflects the Jewish custom. Now as the day of the crucifixion comes to an end, one more detail is added. "Mary Magdalene and Mary the mother of Joses saw where the body was laid." (15:47) Their knowledge is essential to Mark's account since as the story unfolds there must be someone at hand who knows where Jesus lies buried.

II. THE DAY OF THE SUN

The "day of Saturn," the Jewish sabbath, passes without incident. "When the sabbath was over, Mary Magdalene, and Mary the mother of James, and Salome bought spices, so that they might go and anoint him. And very early on the first day of the week, when the sun had risen, they went to the tomb." (16:1–2) The gap between Jesus' burial and the final scene of the Gospel is bridged by the three women. "They had been saying to one another, 'Who will roll away the stone for us from the entrance to the tomb?' When they looked up, they saw that the stone, which was very large, had already been rolled back." (16:3–4)

On entering the tomb, they are confronted by "a young man, dressed in a white robe, sitting on the right side; and they were alarmed." (16:5) Mark does not identify the "young man." There is no reason to believe that the figure is an "angel" or spiritual being of any sort. He seeks to reassure the women. "Do not be alarmed; you are looking for Jesus of Nazareth, who was crucified. He has been raised; he is not here. Look, there is the place they laid him." (16:6) There are no witnesses to Jesus' resurrection. The succeeding evangelists give different accounts of the discovery of the empty tomb (Matthew 28:1ff; Luke 24:1ff; John 20:1ff).

The first Gospel ends with the message of the young man and the enigmatic flight of the women: "But go, tell his disciples and Peter that he is going ahead of you to Galilee; there you will see him, just as he told you." (16:7) Jesus' followers were told this earlier: "But after I am raised up, I will go before you to Galilee." (14:28) Apparently, the words of the young man do not reach either Peter or the disciples: "So [the women] went out and fled from the tomb, for terror and amazement had seized them; and they said nothing to anyone, for they were afraid." (16:8)

Mark and his community would certainly have been aware of the post-resurrection appearances of Jesus to his disciples. The apostle Paul relates "that [Jesus] appeared to Cephas, then to the twelve. Then he appeared to more than five hundred brothers and sisters at one time, most of whom are still alive, though some have died. Then he appeared to James, then to all the apostles. Last of all, as to one untimely born, he appeared also to me." (I Corinthians 15:5–8) Why then does Mark omit the appearances of Jesus after his resurrection, appearances the succeeding Gospels describe, often in some detail?

A possible reason would be that the return of a "heavenly" Jesus, appearing to his followers, would undermine Mark's emphasis that Jesus was genuinely human and not a divinity in disguise. Norman Perrin suggests another explanation: "For Mark the only state of things between the resurrection and parousia is that brief interim period in which Christians learn the meaning of true discipleship ... all in anticipation of the judgment and glory of the parousia." (*The Resurrection Narratives*, p. 34) The only manifestation of the resurrected Jesus with any significance for Mark is that of his return when "they will see 'the Son of Man coming in clouds' with great power and glory. Then he will send out the angels, and gather his elect from the four winds, from the ends of the earth to the ends of heaven." (13:26–27)

If the first Gospel seems to us to conclude abruptly we must again recall that Mark and his community lived in expectation of Jesus' return in glory. It would be they, not the high priest, who would see the promise fulfilled: "You will see the Son of Man 'seated at the right hand of the Power,' and 'coming with the clouds of heaven.'" (14:62) Earlier appearances of Jesus only foreshadowed the parousia.

STUDY QUESTIONS

1. What was the charge against Jesus in the presence of Pilate?
2. Why was such an accusation a sensitive matter for the Roman Christians?
3. How is Pilate pictured in the Marcan account of Jesus' trial?
4. What might the first Gospel be stressing in Jesus' being mocked by the Roman soldiers?
5. What figure from the Isaian prophecies does the Gospel of Mark bring to mind during Jesus' torments?
6. Which Psalm appears to have influenced the Marcan account of Jesus' execution?
7. What three groups mock Jesus while he is on the cross?
8. How is the reader to understand the final words of Jesus, *Eloi, Eloi, lema sabachthani*?
9. What is the significance of the tearing of the temple's curtain?
10. Why would a centurion be especially meaningful for the readers of Mark's Gospel?
11. What crucial role do the women at the crucifixion fulfill?
12. What may have been Joseph of Arimathea's motive in burying Jesus?
13. To what are the women witnesses?
14. How is the abrupt ending of the first Gospel explained?

Chapter Fourteen

AFTERWORD

I. THE COMMUNITY OF MARK

With the conclusion of the first Gospel, our knowledge of Mark's church ends. On two occasions in the first Gospel, the reader is told of a promised post-resurrection appearance of Jesus in Galilee, once by Jesus himself: "But after I am raised up, I will go before you to Galilee" (14:28), and again by the young man at the tomb: "But go, tell his disciples and Peter that he is going ahead of you to Galilee; there you will see him, just as he told you." (16:7) In the light of these passages, some have proposed that Mark's community went to Palestine to await Jesus' promised return. If true, it would not have been the last time that Christians abandoned their regular lives and went to some location or other, there hoping to meet Jesus at the parousia.

However, Mark's parable of the household living in expectation of the master's return (13:34–36) may have been an admonition against just such a possibility. In the story, the man "leaves home and puts his slaves in charge, each with his work." (13:34) The implication is that the Christian is to continue life as usual while awaiting the end, but always alert and ready to greet the returning Jesus: "And what I say to you I say to all: Keep awake." (13:37)

Now, one can live in such expectation for only so long. In time, Mark's community must have come to the realization that the parousia lay farther in the future than had been thought. We have posited that other more conservative Christian communities existed in Rome and elsewhere. Less apocalyptic in their expectations, Mark's churches would have come into line with these more "mainstream" communities of the empire. With the Marcan Christians would have come the first Gospel.

II. THE OTHER COMMUNITIES

It was mentioned earlier that a rival, more conservative Christian church coexisted in Rome with Mark's community. There is evidence of their presence as we can see from an observation of Raymond Brown: "Two works, I Peter from Rome and Hebrews written to Rome, supply some information about Rome in the period between the Epistle of Paul to the Romans (*ca.* 58) and *I Clement* from Rome (*ca.* 96). Neither of these intermediary works can be assigned a certain date, but one cannot be far wrong in placing them in the period between the late 60s and the early 90s, with the suspicion that both may belong to the 80s." (*Antioch and Rome*, p. 128) They would put us very close to the period in which Mark's Gospel was written.

What I Peter and Hebrews reveal is a Christian community that more reflects Paul's letter to the Romans than Mark's Gospel. Brown observes that three themes unite these documents. "These significant strains of thought are: first, a frequent use of Jewish cultic language; second, an insistence on obedience to civil authority; and third, an increasing articulation of church structure." (*Ibid.* p. 136) These Christians then were closer to the Jewish traditions than Mark and do not appear to have expected a proximate parousia as did Mark's Christians. Concern for church structure is not a characteristic of those for whom the world is about to end. A greater concern for church structure is indicated by the attribution of I Peter to the leader of the apostles, the figure that Mark puts in so bad a light.

We see the same in the pastoral letters, Titus and I and II Timothy. These documents attributed to Paul actually originated in the late first century. Though they do not directly reflect the situation in Rome, they too show Christians of concerns differing from those of Mark. "What the author of the Pastorals did intend was to urge church leaders to value and maintain ecclesial and societal structure and order." (Robert A. Wild, S.J., *NJBC*, p. 893a) We see in the pastorals no expectation of the parousia. The focus of these documents is on a stable church administration: As we saw above, when the proximate end of the world is anticipated these are not matters of great concern.

Writing at the beginning of the second century, the unknown author of II Peter asks the rhetorical question: "Where is the promise of his coming? For ever since our ancestors died, all things continue as they were from the beginning of creation!" (3:4) In explaining the delay of the parousia, the writer reminds his reader, "But do not ignore this one fact, beloved, that with the Lord one day is like a thousand years, and a thousand years are like one day. The Lord is not slow about his promise, as some think of slowness, but is patient with you, not wanting any to perish, but all to come to repentance." (3:8–9) II Peter was the last written of the documents that make up the New Testament. Expectation of an imminent parousia had now faded. Nevertheless, throughout the subsequent history of Christianity, it would flare up again and again fade away.

III. THE SUCCEEDING GOSPELS

A. The Prestige of Mark

None of the above mentioned New Testament documents shows any direct influence of Mark's Gospel. Nevertheless, there certainly were Christian communities that shared the expectation of the parousia. While expectations ran high, Mark must have enjoyed considerable prestige. In spite of the expenses incurred in copying and recopying a manuscript, the work must have circulated widely. Yet when the anticipation faded the first Gospel couldn't simply be discarded. There was far more to it than just a prediction of Jesus' return in glory. The first Gospel had given readers a forceful vision of Jesus as well as a record of his words and deeds.

Mark's influence is testified to by the composition of two other Gospels within ten or fifteen years, each originating in a different part of the empire and incorporating different traditions. We have seen already how the Gospels of Matthew and Luke varied from Mark in many areas. What concerns us here is that they also reflect the change in attitude toward the parousia. Fredriksen observes, "By the time Matthew and Luke write, the destruction of the temple was well in the past, and things had continued much as before. It could not, therefore, be a signal of the beginning of the End. But Mark, writing shortly after 70, could not have known this...." (*Op. cit.* p. 51)

B. Matthew

As with Mark, the actual author of the second Gospel is unknown. Father Brown identifies him as "a reflective Jewish Christian and a former scribe." (*The Churches the Apostles Left Behind*, p. 126) The place of origin for the Gospel is usually taken to be Antioch in Syria. The city's Christian community was second only to that of Jerusalem in renown. It was this community that had recruited and sent forth Paul on his missionary journeys. Peter was also there (Galatians 2:11). In Antioch, Jesus' followers were first called "Christians." (Acts 11:26)

The regard for the first Gospel can be seen in the fact that Matthew incorporates six hundred of the six hundred and sixty verses in Mark, usually word for word. At various points Matthew inserts additional material drawn from the traditions of his own community and a tradition he shares with Luke.[1] Much of what is added consists of Jesus' teachings. Facing an indefinite future, Christians will need more detailed guidance. The material Matthew adds fulfills such a purpose.

The community of Matthew is not living in anticipation of the parousia. Fredriksen notes: "But [Matthew's] attention and energies focus on the mystery of the cosmic Son of Man who comes down and goes up, not an apocalyptic Son of Man who goes away and will return." (*Op. cit.* p. 43) Jesus meets his disciples in Galilee and sends them on their mission: "And Jesus came and said to them, 'All authority in heaven and on earth has been given to me. Go therefore and make disciples of all nations, baptizing them in the name of the Father and of the Son and of the Holy Spirit, and teaching them to obey everything that I have commanded you. And remember, I am with you always, to the end of the age.'" (28:18–19) The implication is that "the end of the age" lies in the distant future.

C. Luke

The third Gospel was written about the same time as Matthew. Again, we do not know the name of the author. Tradition only identifies him as Luke. Someone by that name is mentioned in letters attributed to Paul. (Colossians 4:14; II Timothy 4:11; Philemon 24) The author is the most skillful of the New Testament writers. With the material from Mark he blends a tradition he shares with Matthew and traditions preserved by his own community. Moreover, to his Gospel, Luke added the work known as the Acts of the Apostles, which relates the spread of the Christian message after the death and resurrection of Jesus. Fredriksen points out:

> Further, [Luke] allays many of the tensions inherent in preserving an initially apocalyptic tradition in the face of an empirical disconfirmation of its central prophecy, for the world had not ended. Finally, it indicates a particular consciousness of the future of the new community, a deeschatologized, this worldly future. Hence Luke does not include the Son of Man, a term with strong apocalyptic associations in the narrative catena of Christological titles at the beginning of his gospel. Christian apocalyptic hope had no place in Luke's theology.... (*Op. cit.* p. 35)

At the close of Luke's Gospel the risen Jesus tells his disciples that "... repentance and forgiveness of sins is to be proclaimed in [the Messiah's] name to all nations, beginning from Jerusalem. You are witnesses of these things." (24:47–48) Then at the beginning of Acts, we have Jesus reminding his followers that " ... you will be my witnesses in Jerusalem, in all Judea and Samaria, and to the ends of the earth." (1:8) Jesus then ascends into the heavens, a scene unique to Luke. Given the challenge they now faced, these followers could not have expected the parousia to occur in the near future. It should be noted that when, in the second century, an ending was added to the Gospel of Mark (16:9–20), the language of the passage most closely resembles that of Luke 24.

IV. MARK'S ACHIEVEMENT

The Christian community that gave us the first Gospel does disappear over the horizon of history as the followers of Jesus began their long turbulent trek down through the centuries. Mark was obviously premature in his effort to prepare his community for the parousia. Yet, this in no way diminishes his achievement. He gave a new meaning to the Good News, Paul's term for Jesus' message. In doing so, Mark gave rise to a form of Christian religious literature that would take its place at the head of those documents forming the core of the Christian tradition, the New Testament. As stated earlier, the Gospel of Mark is truly a revolutionary achievement.

In the current arrangement of the New Testament, Mark's work is sandwiched between the two evangelists which he inspired in so many ways. Mark is not the first innovator to be overshadowed by his successors. The Jesus of Matthew and the Jesus of Luke may have a greater grip on our imaginations. Nevertheless, they drew upon the portrait first outlined by Mark, the Jesus so human, yet divine, Son of God, yet Son of Man, wonderworker and teacher. Mark's successors built upon that image; they never obscured it.

V. IN CLOSING

We have tried to look through Mark's Gospel to the Christian community in which it originated. Given that almost two millennia separate us from them, our task seemed at first formidable, if not impossible. Shopkeepers, tradesmen, artisans, for the most part, these dwellers in the empire's capital lived lives quite different from ours. One would expect their understanding of Jesus' message to be much different from ours. They, after all, were believers sharing an atmosphere saturated with paganism in all its bizarre forms. There were shrines to a variety of deities in every home and on virtually every street corner. The most impressive of the buildings found everywhere in the city were temples to Rome's gods and goddesses. The smoke of constant sacrifices must have added to the pungency of the city.

Christianity was little known and less understood. With no legal standing and no exemptions to the laws demanding participation in the state religion, these Christians were well aware of the cost their faith could demand of them. The practice of their religion exacted a price, for some a high price, since the Christian was cut off from participation in the social and political life of the city. Also theirs was a Christianity without that development in doctrine that has spanned almost twenty centuries.

Yet for all of what has been said, our predecessors in first century Rome are no strangers. After all, their Greco-Roman culture is one we share with them. Our language, architecture, even our laws hark back to theirs. Most importantly, we are linked to them by sharing the same basic faith in Jesus of Nazareth. The full measure of the first evangelist's success is that his work has come down to us as a guide to that faith. Layers of history and doctrinal development lie between ourselves and Mark's community, but their faith shines through and continues to enrich our generation as it has for those who preceded us and will continue for those who follow us.

STUDY QUESTIONS

1. What might have happened to the Marcan community?
2. What two New Testament documents give evidence of other Christian communities in Rome?
3. What are the possible characteristics of these communities?
4. What picture of other Christian communities is presented by the pastoral letters attributed to Paul?
5. What explanation does II Peter give for the delay of the parousia?
6. In what way does the Gospel of Matthew change the emphasis of Mark in the matter of the parousia?
7. How does the Gospel of Luke do the same?
8. What are the accomplishments of the first Gospel?
9. What links us to Christians whose faith is expressed in the Gospel of Mark?

Notes

PROLOGUE

[1]From the Founding of the City (of Rome).

[2]We will follow the current convention of using C.E. (Current Era) to indicate dates after the birth of Christ and B.C.E. (Before the Current Era) for the dates prior to his birth.

PREFACE

[1]The term widely used by Christians, the Old Testament, conveys a characterization of something being *passé*. I prefer the usage, the Hebrew Bible. Keep in mind, however, that the Scriptures used by the Jewish people do not contain books and passages found in the Scripture used by Roman Catholics. The reason for this will be dealt with later.

1. THE FIRST GOSPEL

[1]It took its name from the tradition that it was prepared by seventy-two scholars. By this time the Jews had come under the influence of the Greek culture. Books and passages of books originally written in Greek and not found in the Hebrew Bible were included in the Septuagint.

[2]Following the conquest and destruction of Jerusalem in the sixth century B.C.E., and the exile of many Jews to Babylon, there were groups of Jews who migrated elsewhere. Over the following centuries, more Jews did the same until, by the beginning of the Current Era, most Jews lived outside of Palestine. These were called the "diaspora" from the Greek for "dispersion."

[3]The English language reflects the Anglo-Saxon *gōd-spel*, meaning "good tidings" or "good news." In contrast, the Romance languages, French, Italian and Spanish, reflect *eu-angelion*, the Greek for "good news." Translations of the New Testament vary in how they render the Greek *eu-angelion*, sometimes using "gospel" and, at others, "good news."

[4]In the Septuagint, the Greek word *KYRIOS*, meaning "LORD," is substituted for *YHWH* in the text of the Hebrew Bible.

[5]References to biblical documents will be in plain text; other references will be in italics.

[6]Written by the same author as the Gospel of Luke, the Acts of the Apostles traces the growth of early Christianity, with an emphasis on the career of the apostle Paul.

[7]*The New Jerusalem Biblical Commentary.*

[8]Vatican hill is the site of present-day St. Peter's Basilica. The obelisk at the center of St. Peter's Square once adorned the emperor's race track.

[9]Josephus (37–c. 100 C.E.) had been a Jewish commander in the war who later defected to the Romans. His account of the conflict betrays some bias reflecting his new allegiance.

2. THE GRANDEUR THAT WAS ROME

[1]This appears to have been the situation with Paul. The crucial nature of Roman citizenship in the empire can be seen from his career as accounted in Acts (16:37–38; 22:25–29; 23:27).

3. CHRISTIANITY IN ROME

[1]"It was in Antioch that the disciples were first called 'Christians.'" (Acts 11:26) We do not know whether the first followers of Jesus to arrive in Rome were designated by this title.

[2]Modern scholarship generally agrees that Paul wrote or dictated I Thessalonians, Galatians, Philippians, I and II Corinthians, Romans and Philemon. The remaining letters in the Pauline corpus are by other authors and were later attributed to Paul.

[3]"Church" derives from the late Greek word *kyriakon* meaning "of the Lord."

[4]The expression to "break bread" was an early Christian designation of the celebration of the eucharist, as we can see more clearly in "They devoted themselves to the apostles' teaching and fellowship, to the breaking of bread and the prayers." (Acts 2:42)

[5]These were three-person couches arranged on the four sides of a table in the Roman style dining room. They also doubled as beds if needed.

[6]In Rome the churches of Santa Susanna and of San Clemente were originally designated as the churches of Gaius and of Clementine, respectively.

[7]Excavations in the crypt of Santa Susanna, Rome's church for the American community, also reveals the presence of an earlier residence. Again,

it was most likely a house church on which was erected a fourth century church building. It appears to have been connected with the Gaius family.

[8]For details of these discoveries, see *A Short Guide to St. Clement's* by Leonard Boyle O.P., Rome: Collegio San Clemente, 1990.

[9]The architectural model chosen for these churches was that of the *basilicae*, the type of structure that housed the law courts.

[10]The glossolalia, the practice of making audible, but unintelligible sounds, as a manifestation of the religious spirit. Paul had hesitations about the phenomenon but did not ban it. See I Corinthians 14:1–28.

4. MARK'S CHRISTIANS

[1]The "family of Caesar" was not made up of the emperor's relatives but was something resembling the empire's civil service. Such functionaries, often freedmen, had access to both wealth and power.

[2]It is generally agreed that the original manuscript of the first Gospel ended at 16:8. The additional verses we find in current versions of Mark were added later.

5. LEADERSHIP AND RIVALRY

[1]The Essenes were a dissident sect of Jews having communities in many cities of the Empire. They are associated with the documents known as the "Dead Sea Scrolls." The sect gradually died out after 70 C.E.

[2]Peter is from the Latin *Petros*, meaning "Rock." In Paul's letters he is also called *Cephas,* the Grecized form of the Aramaic *Kepa,* also meaning "rock."

[3]"The Jewish scribe in New Testament times is the scholar and intellectual of Judaism.... His scholarship was the knowledge of the Law...." (McKenzie, *op. cit.* p. 780b) With one exception (12:28f) the scribes in Mark appear as hostile to Jesus.

6. THE PAROUSIA AND THE SON OF MAN

[1]At one point Mark mentions, "The Pharisees went out and immediately conspired with the Herodians against him, how to destroy [Jesus]." (3:6) However, the first evangelist does not indicate that the threat was carried out by either group.

[2]From the Greek for "presence" or "arrival."

[3]Scholars agree that the prophecy of Isaiah is the work of three authors

writing at different times. The third of these wrote after the Jews had returned from exile.

[4]Written by an unknown author (*c.* 164 B.C.E.) the book of Daniel sought to encourage the Judeans in their struggle against the efforts of Antiochus IV Epiphanes (175–164 B.C.E.) to suppress the Jewish religion. It is an example of what we might call "historical fiction." The characters are real, being drawn from period of the exile (the sixth century B.C.E.). The described events, however, are imaginary. The account of a young Jew's efforts to remain faithful to his religion is meant to encourage the reader to do the same.

[5]The Aramaic is *bar nasha.* The literal meaning is "son of man" but can simply be a way of indicating "a human being."

7. CHRIST AND SON OF GOD

[1]The Greek *Christos* translates the Hebrew *Messiah,* meaning "anointed one."

[2]Roughly from 100 B.C.E. to 55 C.E., i.e. from the completion of II Maccabees to I Thessalonians.

[3]As to the question of what Jesus himself claimed, we have Raymond Brown's conclusion: "I judge it plausible that during Jesus' lifetime some of his followers thought him to be the Messiah, i.e. the expected anointed king of the House of David who would rule over God's people. Jesus, confronted with this identification, responded ambivalently...." (*The Death of Jesus, op. cit.* p. 480)

[4]In the previous century, when Spartacus and his followers were executed, the roads leading to Rome were lined for miles with the crosses of the unfortunate victims.

[5]The city would have been well-known to Mark's readers. Vespasian headquartered there at the beginning of the Jewish war and Titus celebrated his triumph there as well. (Josephus, *op. cit.* pp. 225, 376)

[6]Interestingly, Mark reflects the Jewish reluctance to speak the name of God and so the high priest used the circumlocution, "Son of the Blessed One."

[7]In his commentary on Philippians, Brendan Byrne, S.J., speaks of "the widespread view that Paul supports his exhortation to selflessness by quoting a hymn composed independently of Philippians." (*NJBC,* p. 794b)

[8]It is a testimony to the vividness of Mark's story that it has inspired both a play (Oscar Wilde) and an opera (Richard Strauss).

[9]Paul himself encountered disciples of John. (Acts 18:24–25; 19:1–5)

[10]The image is not that of a dove itself, but of some manifestation of the Spirit hovering like a dove.

8. DIVINE AND YET HUMAN

[1]"I prefer to translate *techton* as 'woodworker' rather than as the popular 'carpenter' because the latter term has acquired a somewhat restricted sense in the contemporary American workplace, with its ever increasing specialization.... Besides carpentry in this sense, Jesus would have made various pieces of furniture, such as beds, tables, stools, and lampstands, as well as boxes, cabinets, and chests for storage." (Meier, *op. cit.* pp. 280–281)

[2]Mark's references to Jesus' brothers and sisters (3:31–32; 6:2–3) have been the subject of much debate over the centuries, especially in view of the church's teaching on the perpetual virginity of Mary. However, Mark knows nothing of this. In fact, Jesus' being part of an extended family serves the evangelist's emphasis on the humanity of Jesus. Their failure to accept him for what he was also fits Mark's theme, which we will come to later, of Jesus' total abandonment. In the second and third centuries C.E., when the reality of Jesus' humanity was being challenged, its supporters appealed to Mark (see Meier, *op. cit.* pp. 329–330). Paul also refers to Jesus' "brothers." (Galatians 1:19; I Corinthians 9:5) Was Jesus married? If Mark had any knowledge of it, he would most likely have used such a fact to further humanize Jesus.

[3]Recent excavations in Palestine discovered the corpse of one who had been crucified. A spike had been driven through the victim's heels, indicating that his legs had been pulled up under him for support, thus lengthening his time of agony.

[4]Scholarship regards the three letters attributed to John as written by a single person several years later than the Gospel.

9. THE WONDERWORKER

[1]In some translations of the New Testament "miracle" is used to translate the Greek *dynamis*. The better equivalent would be "deed of power."

[2]A very ancient middle eastern name of an evil spirit.

[3]A heavenly being who first appears in the story of Job (2:1–4; 6–7) as his adversary. Only in later Jewish speculation does he become the leader of the forces of evil.

[4]On the same site, there has been a hospital since the middle ages.

10. THE TEACHER AND HIS TEACHINGS

[1]The Greek word *parabole* is used to translate the Aramaic *masal*, meaning "wise saying."

[2]Discovered in 1945, *The Gospel of Thomas* purports to be a collection of Jesus' sayings and may have originated as early as the late first century C.E. Some of the quotations may actually be more authentic than the version in the Gospels.

[3]"Kingdom" is perhaps not the best translation of either the Hebrew *malkut* or the Greek *basileia*. It is not a designation of territory as "kingdom" might imply, but one of "rule" or "reign."

11. THE HOLY WEEK: PART ONE

[1]The English actor, Alec McCowen, toured doing a dramatic reading of "St. Mark's Gospel" as a stage presentation. A videotape of the performance is available.

[2]The "cursing of the fig tree" (11:13–14,20) is better viewed as a parable in action than as a deed of power.

[3]Mark does not directly identify the days. However, the reader is told that the fourth day of the week is "two days before the Passover" (14:1) and the Passover is "the day before the sabbath." (15:42) Thus the first day of Holy Week is the day of the sun.

[4]Much later Christians will choose December 25, then the equinox and "birthday" of the sun, as the day on which to celebrate the birth of Jesus.

[5]The Roman weekly cycle was inherited from the Babylonians and each day was dedicated to one of the planets. As a reminder of how Mark's readers would have experienced the "holy week," in what follows the days will be given their pagan names.

[6]The meaning of "Hosanna."

[7]Thanks to archeological excavations, today's visitors to Jerusalem can see several of these large stones lying at the foot of the temple mount, just as they have been for almost two millennia.

[8]As noted earlier, it is generally agreed that the original manuscript of Mark ended with verse 16:8.

12. THE HOLY WEEK: PART TWO

[1]It is Wednesday. The chronology can be confusing. Mark tells the reader that Jesus died on "the day before the sabbath." (15:42) That day, Friday, was also the feast of Passover. For Mark, who is following the Roman cus-

tom of beginning a day at midnight, it is two days away. For the Jews, whose day began at sunset, Passover started the next evening with the celebration of the traditional seder.

[2]Matthew and Luke follow Mark's pattern, but in John's Gospel the "Last Supper" is clearly not a Passover meal (13:1).

[3]" 'Fled' may be too weak a translation, for there is a note of abandonment." (Brown, *op. cit.* p. 287)

[4]In Mark's Greek, the word used is *syn-edrion*.

[5]Mark's Gentile readers would have been familiar with this gesture as an expression of grief and anger: "In his *History* (54.14.1–2) Cassio Dio tells us of Lucinius Regulus who tore his apparel (*estheta*) publicly in the Roman Senate when he discovered he was not on the list of selected members. The Emperor Augustus tore his apparel on hearing of the defeat of Varus in Germany (56.23.1)." (Brown, *op. cit.* p. 517)

[6]The "cock crows" could also refer to trumpet blasts that marked the hours of the night watch in a military encampment. (Cf. Brown, *Ibid.* p. 606)

[7]Isaiah 42:1–4; 49:1–6; 50:4–9; 52:13–53:12.

13. THE HOLY WEEK: PART THREE

[1]The prisoner's name is strange, meaning "son of the father."

[2]Apparently, it was the common practice to flog the victim prior to his crucifixion.

[3]This could be a parody of the shout that would greet the emperor: "Hail! Victor! Emperor!"

[4]What Simon would have carried was only the cross beam (*patibulum*), which would later be placed on the upright section (*staticulum*) already in place where the victim would be executed.

[5]Recent archeological excavations have shown that the site of Jesus' execution was an abandoned quarry outside the walls of Jerusalem. In the center was a mound of unquarried rock perhaps reminiscent of a skull. In the quarry's walls were tombs. (Cf. Brown, *op. cit.* p. 938)

[6]The remains of a victim of crucifixion have been discovered in Palestine. A nail had been driven through his heels to fasten him to the cross.

[7]The original text has "third hour," "sixth hour" and "ninth hour" (see v. 53) reflecting the Roman division of daylight, i.e. dawn to dusk, into twelve "hours." Each of these divisions would vary in length during the year.

[8]Actually, such a mistake would have not been possible in the original semitic. But Mark's Gentile readers would not have known that. (See Brown's detailed discussion, *ibid.* pp. 1058–1063)

[9]Actually, "sour wine" (*oxos*) was a cheap form of wine and was generally regarded as soldiers' drink, so it would have been at hand. Offering it to
Jesus may have been an act of kindness preserved in the tradition Mark
received.

14. AFTERWORD

[1]The material that Matthew and Luke share is called "Q" from the
German *Quelle* or "Source." If we accept the premise of Burton L. Mack in
his The *Lost Gospel*, the tradition represented in "Q" is the very earliest
record of Jesus' teachings.

Bibliography

ROMAN LIFE AND CULTURE

Barrow, R. H., *The Romans*. New York: Penguin Books, 1986

Carcopino, Jérôme, *Daily Life in Ancient Rome*. New Haven and London: Yale University Press, 1940

Christ, Carl, *The Romans*. Berkeley and Los Angeles: University of California Press, 1984

Coulanges, Numa Denis Fustel, *The Ancient City*. Garden City: Doubleday and Company, Inc.

Cumont, Franz, *Oriental Religions in Roman Paganism*. New York: Dover Publications, 1956

Grant, Michael, *The World of Rome*. New York: New American Library, 1960

Lefkowitz, Mary R. and Fant, Maureen B., *Women's Life in Greece and Rome*. Baltimore: The Johns Hopkins University Press, 1982

MacMullen, Ramsay, *Roman Social Relations*. New Haven and London: Yale University Press, 1974

Shelton, Jo-Ann, *As the Romans Did*. New York: Oxford University Press, 1988

THE EARLY CHRISTIANS

Branick, Vincent P., *The House Church in the Writings of Paul*. Wilmington, Delaware: Michael Glazier, 1989

Brown, Raymond E., *The Churches the Apostles Left Behind*. New York: Paulist Press, 1984

—and Meier, John P., *Antioch & Rome*. New York: Paulist Press, 1983

Fox, Robin Lane, *Pagans and Christians*. San Francisco: Harper & Row, 1986

Meeks, Wayne A., *The First Urban Christians*. New Haven and London: Yale University Press, 1983

THE ANCIENT HISTORIANS AND WRITERS

Josephus, *The Jewish War*. New York: Penguin Classics, 1981

Juvenal, *The Satires of Juvenal*. Bloomington: Indiana University Press, 1958

Suetonius, *The Twelve Caesars*. New York: Penguin Classics, 1989

Tacitus, *The Annals of Imperial Rome*. New York: Penguin Classics, 1971

—*The Histories*. New York: Penguin Classics, 1986

JESUS

Crossan, John Dominic, *The Historical Jesus*. San Francisco: Harper, 1991

Fredricksen, Paula, *From Jesus to Christ*. New Haven and London: Yale University Press, 1988

Grant, Michael, *Jesus*. New York: Charles Scribner's Sons, 1977

Meier, John P., *A Marginal Jew*. New York: Doubleday, 1991

Vermes, Geza, *Jesus the Jew*. Philadelphia: Fortress Press, 1973

SCRIPTURE COMMENTARIES

Achtemeier, Paul J., *Proclamation Commentaries: Mark*. Philadelphia: Fortress Press, 1975

Brown, Raymond E., *The Death of the Messiah*. New York: Doubleday, 1994

Cunningham, Phillip J., *Exploring Scripture: How the Bible Came To Be*. New York and Mahwah: Paulist Press, 1992

Dodd, C. H., *The Parables of the Kingdom*. Glasgow: William Collins Sons & Co., 1961

Jeremias, Joachim, *The Parables of Jesus*. New York: Charles Scribner's Sons, 1963

The New Jerome Biblical Commentary (NJBC). Englewood Cliffs: Prentice-Hall, 1990

Perkins, Pheme, *Reading the New Testament*. Mahwah: Paulist Press, 1988

Perrin, Norman, *Rediscovering the Teaching of Jesus*. New York: Harper & Row, Publishers, 1976

—*The Resurrection Narratives*. London: SCM Press, 1977

Young, Brad H., *Jesus and His Jewish Parables*. Mahwah: Paulist Press, 1989

MISCELLANEOUS

de Vaux, Roland, *Ancient Israel*. New York: McGraw-Hill Book Company, Inc., 1961

The Gospel of Thomas, translation by Marvin Meyer. San Francisco: Harper San Francisco, 1993

Jeremias, Joachim, *Jerusalem in the Times of Jesus*. New York: Fortress Press, 1969

Mack, Burton L., *The Lost Gospel*. San Francisco: Harper San Francisco, 1993

McKenzie, S.J., John L., *Dictionary of the Bible*. New York: Macmillan Publishing Co. Inc., 1965

Warington, B. H., *Nero: Reality and Legend*. New York: W. W. Norton & Company Inc., 1969

Index